RIGHT WING, WRONG BIRD

Why the Tactics of the Religious Right Won't Fly
With Most Conservative Christians

Right Wing, Wrong Bird
www.rightwingwrongbird.com

© 2006 JOEL C. HUNTER
ISBN 0-9786783-0-3

Published by Distributed Church Press,
530 Dog Track Road, Longwood, Florida 32750

Unless otherwise noted, Scripture quotations taken from the
New American Standard Bible®, Copyright © 1960, 1962, 1963, 1968,
1971, 1972, 1973, 1975, 1977, 1995 by The Lockman Foundation.
Used by permission. (www.Lockman.org) Quotations marked KJV are
from the King James Version of the Bible.

CONTENTS

To Becky—my wife, best friend and editor at so many levels!

Thanks also to Robert Andrescik, a great communications director and encourager. His expertise and ideas for the book were an invaluable contribution. Thanks to Nathan Clark and DeDe Caruso for their work on the design of the book. Thanks to Melissa Bogdany, Audrey Laird, and Joel D. Hunter, M.D. for their help with the editing.

And thanks to the Northland Elder Board, and the great staff at the church, all of whom are so good at what they do that they can lend their senior pastor to such an effort as this. Thanks also to the Northland congregation for their devotion to serving Christ in the world.

Also, thanks to my friends in the National Association of Evangelicals and the World Evangelical Alliance, who extend my vision of the local church.

PREFACE

Here are seven reasons the current strategy of the religious right won't fly with most conservative Christians:

1. Wrong tone (too polarizing/enemy creating)

Ideas compete; radicals attack. Christians can and should debate, but leaders of the religious right have fostered a personal war. Whereas creating emergencies and enemies is good for media ratings and fundraising, it is a turnoff to reasonable people who want a solution rather than a shouting match.

A better approach is obvious and needed: respectful and reasonable competition of ideas, trusting that the Spirit of truth will guide conservative Christians to effective action.

2. Too limited in emphasis and issues

The religious right has settled in on a few "below the belt" issues. Though being pro-life will remain the premier issue before all others (it is premature to focus on a better society if you don't protect individual existence), and though sex-based problems from pornography to redefining marriage are epidemic, other issues are just as biblical.

A better approach is this: expand our biblical and moral obedience to help Christians address issues such as poverty, disease, pollution, and injustice.

3. Focused on political wins rather than spiritual results

The religious right has settled for the assumption of politics: "If we win, the country will be better."

A deeper understanding is this: the greatest result of a political process is not better social policy; it is more Christlike and responsible people. We can impact government, but political involvement should be a matter of spiritual growth. The mentalities of winning and of growing into spiritually mature people are not identical.

4. Too linked to one political party

For the most part, the religious right has been limited to the Republican Party. A voice of biblical values cannot be in the pocket of one party.

5. Not deep enough intellectually

What are the scriptural and philosophical foundations of

the political positions we hold? Will reflex reactions to hot-button issues really provide the long-term and thoughtful guidance that our society needs? Unless Christians can be taught to explain their values and their voting decisions in an intellectually credible way to those who disagree, we will not create understanding … let alone growth.

6. Not effective at mobilizing churches

The religious right is a parachurch group rather than a church-oriented group. What that means is this: While there are a fraction of churches and pastors involved in the public square, the most powerful and organized part of Christianity has yet to be engaged.

To be fully effective we must focus on the church. We can train pastors to help their congregation members live as Christian citizens, instead of just calling individual Christians to fight societal issues and ills.

7. Aim is not service, but power

From a political standpoint, what is the difference between the religious right and every other power group wanting to promote its own agenda in government? Answer: none that we can see.

What should be the difference between a group of people who are like Christ and every other group? Answer: He came to serve, not to be served.

So, we are looking for new leadership, but no "WACKOs" need apply. What is a "WACKO"?

Wants only what is good for his or her own group

Angry; hot-button issues oriented

Christian in name, but not Christlike in nature

Knocks others who are different

Only interested in winning, not in growing spiritually

INTRODUCTION

Something was different about Dr. Stanley I. Shoemaker as he stood behind his high pulpit that Sunday. I looked around First Methodist Church, Shelby, Ohio, as I did every Sunday as a boy. Everyone looked so perfect. The men were in suits formal enough for a funeral. White collars were more than their categories of work. Those collars were symbols of self-confidence and sophistication.

The ladies lifted their stately heads to the Reverend Doctor in the pulpit. The fruit on their hats tilted ever so slightly upwards. I looked to Dr. Shoemaker, too, for another distinguished but indistinguishable message. His robed arms braced him as he leaned toward us. The tone of his voice braced us all as he spoke the opening words. Then Dr. Shoemaker let go of a sermon the likes of which I had never heard. Gone were the usual long, academic words like *redemptive intent* and *eschatological hope* and *alienation*. Here came words like *sin* and *repent* and *you*.

Men folded their arms across their chests. Women let their mouths drift open in disbelief. The emotional temperature was rising to the point that the fruit on their hats could have gone the way of cherries jubilee. And then, the ultimate surprise—

Dr. Shoemaker gave an altar call. He asked for any to come forward and confess faith in Christ. The tension was so thick you could have knelt on it. A voice inside me urged me to go. I looked around once more, hoping that someone would lead the way. As the hymn verses pushed on, it was apparent that no one was going to visibly respond. My insides wrestled for a decision, but neither side won during the closing verses and benediction.

Dr. Shoemaker went away discouraged. To my knowledge, he never tried that again at First Church. That Sunday's invitation, however, never left me. It created a hunger within me for the deep and significant matters of life.

Years later I was a freshman at Ohio University. It was the mid-1960s. The United States was making new policies left and right, mostly right. The students were polarized left and right, mostly left. Armed forces had just entered Cambodia. The Civil Rights movement was in full bloom. Students entered into intense political analysis. The student leaders I heard were most eloquent and serious. They spoke of deep and significant issues: of how people ought to be, of how government was so wrong, of what better ideas young people have. Though I was against the extremist factions of the movement, I was drawn into the center that reasoned for solutions and was impassioned for results. I had found my new inspiration. I placed all my hope in political philosophies led by new and improved personalities—like Robert Kennedy and Martin Luther King, Jr.

But a strange thing happened on the way to Utopia. In all of the wonderfully intense idealism, we missed something that could ruin everything. What was it that killed my heroes? What was it that turned the reasoned, positive, uplifting dreams into verbal weapons of cynicism and bitterness? The rhetoric had changed from "this is how to improve what we have now" to "this is how to destroy what we have now." The student leaders began to debate and attack one another. What was it that disintegrated altruism into egotism? A major part of the leaders' solutions had turned into personal ambition. All was being corrupted. What was it that was tainting every good effort?

For the first time I came to realize the social and personal devastation of sin. I marveled at its depth and subtlety. I had heard enough descriptions of it to remember its characteristics. I had remembered something Dr. Shoemaker had said, "Nothing will ever come right in the world until you address the sin in your own heart." I had remembered enough of Dr. Shoemaker's invitation to know the solution.

One night I walked the aisle to a generic altar in the university's Galbreath Chapel. There I responded to Dr. Shoemaker's altar call of years before. Alone in the chapel, I knelt and placed all my confidence in Christ.

I did not abandon hope of an improved political structure. I majored in history and government, though after my experience in the chapel I put them into a new perspective. I knew that depending on improvements in our government to make any major change in people was too simplistic and unrealistic.

As Alexander Solzhenitsyn once said, "Gradually it was disclosed to me that the line dividing good and evil passes not through states, nor between classes, nor between political parties either—but right through every human heart."

The introduction to this book then is both theoretical and personal. My journey was from political idealism, through disillusionment, to the Lord of the universe who is stationed in the heart. I see some evangelical Christians tempted to reverse that order of progress in the name of "practical Christianity." It is especially for those that this book is written.

This book attempts to clarify the important interplay of religion and politics in our society. The potential problem does not lie, as many believe, in mixing religion and politics. The problem comes in mixing them up, in confusing the results of one with the other.

When we talk of religion, we will be talking about Christianity. Yet many of the same principles and cautions could apply to other faiths. When we talk of politics we will be confining most remarks to the electoral process. While the judicial branch of our government is ultimately responsible for defining the meaning of "separation of church and state," the scope of this work is confined to issues concerning elected officials. It must be remembered, though, that election results affect future court decisions.

It is also important to note that both the style and content of this book are intended to serve the thinking believer. It is not intended mainly for the academician, though its theories might interest one. Rather, it is intended for the voter especially interested in understanding these issues and acting on that understanding. As you will read, there is at least as much reason to be active as there is to be careful.

ONE

THE GREAT MIX-UP:

That Bird Won't Fly!

Many of us are apprehensive about the future. Some grave problems afflict our society, and we know it is our responsibility to address them. We could escape our responsibility with some glib Christian cliché like, "I don't know what the future holds, but I know Who holds the future." We have a distinct sense, however, that God calls for our involvement as well as our confidence. Most of us would be glad to take corrective measures if we knew what measures would be most effective.

Many Christians are becoming involved. Led by the evangelicals, we form a religiopolitical team that has grown into a significant force. We are a fervent, focused power in the American political process. There are several groups of Christians with specific political strategies, trying for specific political offices and for specifically religious reasons. That kind of direct, practical action should make Christians feel that we have representation in government and an expressway to involvement when we choose to get active.

But some of us are still apprehensive. It is not that we think these involved evangelicals are wrong. We agree with so much of what they have to say. Yet hopping on the bandwagon does not feel quite right either. We need to do some thinking first.

The religious right has become allied with the political right to form the right wing—a more conservative or, as some would say, reactionary—political force. More subtly, the Christians have theologically unified and confused the biblical forms of government with America's forms.

The religious right has not declined in recent years as some have speculated; it has just become more strident and calcified in its focus. It has developed a strong following on several key issues including abortion and keeping God references in the public square. (Conversely, it has not developed a broader list of concerns well-documented in the Bible, including poverty, injustice, and the environment, which resonate more with younger evangelicals and Catholics.)

The direct threat of redefining marriage, Internet pornography being so accessible to our kids, and other dangers have pushed the religious right into a historically unusual activism in politics. Before this, organized Christian involvement had run in cycles and had been more pronounced on the liberal side of the church. The issues in the 1800s included prison reform, women's rights, and care for the mentally insane. At the turn of the century the issues centered around people victimized by industrialization, such as improved working conditions, the right to strike, housing the homeless. In the 1960s, liberal Christians were instrumental in the civil rights movement and the protest of the Vietnam War.

The conservative side of Christianity has not been politically vocal since the fundamentalists' efforts in prohibition (trying to ban alcohol consumption) and the infamous 1925 Scopes "Monkey Trial" (trying to eliminate teaching the theory of evolution). The embarrassment of those eventual failures sent fundamentalists back to dealing with matters in the church.

In the years before the 1970s, the religiously conservative electorate was more prone to name solutions than details. But things changed decades ago. In the American tradition of pragmatism, the religious right is bonding with the political right to change the nation. What happened?

The Relapse-Religion Connection

Anything that subtracts the tradition of religion from our society frightens concerned evangelicals. Evangelicals are not against abortion simply because we are on the conservative side of issues; we believe it is legalized murder. Evangelicals are not against gay marriage because we are hatemongers; we are against gay marriage because it doesn't fit the pattern laid down in Genesis 2:18-24. We are also against polygamy, polyandry, and bestiality for the same reason. Many Christians believe our laws are beginning to undermine the foundational principles upon which our nation stands.

Evangelicals are not the only ones becoming uneasy with the trends in society. For most Americans, the speed at which things are changing is unnerving. The various "rights" movements have confronted us all with the hazards of "me and my rights" assertiveness. Is this assertiveness simply a continuation of the rugged individualism so necessary for survival in the early (and isolated) years of our country, or is it the kind of individualism that produces isolation and tears apart the fabric of group loyalties? We wonder how extensively public policy can protect the individual without harming the group.

When trends and values differ, one of the results is apprehension. And where should Americans turn with apprehensions about a fast-changing society? The natural answer is that they turn to religion (for old-fashioned values) and to politics (to put the brakes on society's permissiveness). Many are afraid that if both religion and government don't set up firmer standards, America will be like the man who fell into the vat of lanolin—and softened to death. Christians think of an even worse fate than that.

Enter the religious right. Their certainty and simple answers sound so—well, certain and simple. The certainty and simplicity give us a feeling of returning to basic morality.

There is enough Christianity in our country's history to make it a very significant component of our heritage and identity. But history, like Scripture, is open to a variety of interpretations. Several Christian authors have distilled American history in a way that ferments a potent theological statement. In many ways we Christians are thirsty to hear that America has merely "lost her way." In our personal need for security and certainty, we are tempted to assume that what elevates our group is best for the entire nation.

In some respects right-wing political involvement has much in common with old wine. It diminishes somewhat the pain of confusion and makes one feel brave and confident. There are certain ailments of our government that could do with a dose of right-wing involvement. But more than a little of such an influence diminishes capacity. Our body politic was not made to ingest strong, specific religious cures. And the New Testament does not recommend such an overwhelming infusion of Christianity into government.

The Old Testament-New Testament Confusion

One characteristic of evangelicals is our enthusiasm to search the Word of God (the Bible) to apply it directly to current situations. According to Paul, "All Scripture is inspired by God and profitable for teaching, for reproof, for correction, for training in righteousness" (2 Timothy 3:16). And so it is. Yet not every part of the Bible has the same relevance to every situation. Amazingly, some students of the Bible miss the obvious difference between God's way of governing before Christ and His plan after Christ.

In the Old Testament, God used political leadership for people who were given His law. It was appropriate for Israel's maturing process, just as rules and parental force are appropriate for young children. The Scripture clearly states, though, that God was preparing them for another form of government. This would be one that would be in the hearts of people. Jeremiah 31:31, 33 prophesies this new government: " 'Behold, days are coming,' declares the Lord, 'when I will make a new covenant. . . . I will put My law within them, and on their heart I will write it.' " Evangelicals believe that many Jews could not conceive of such a radically new system. The basic assumption among many evangelicals is that a strong reason the Jews do not accept Jesus as the Messiah is because He did not bring political change. These are the same evangelicals who, after they have called the Jews ignorant, are wanting Christ to reign politically!

The confusion comes with the Puritan tradition that assumes America to be the New Israel, a "city set on a hill," as John Winthrop so inspiringly stated. That Old Testament, "new chosen people" imagery might be good for ego gratification, but it is poor exegesis and silly theology. There was only one chosen people. God used Old Testament Israel for His special purposes, to be a blessing to all nations by preparing the world for the grace brought in Christ. God needs no "new Israels." We are His sons and daughters in Christ, not a revised version of the Jews. We are under no compulsion to imitate the government of Old Testament Israel.

God once ruled Israel by law and external government. God now rules Christian people by grace and internal government. John 1:17 states, "For the law was given through Moses; grace and truth were realized through Jesus Christ."

The New Testament does speak to the issue of Christians and government. We are to respect the external government: "Let everyone be in subjection to the governing authorities" (Romans 13:1). We are to cooperate and give our civil duty its due: "Render to Caesar the things that are Caesar's" (Mark 12:17). We are to do such to aid our witness, our influence for Christ. First Peter 2:12-17 is quite clear about our obeying government so that others will see no wrong and "glorify God." Political reform and office, though, are about loving our neighbor, not about getting in power.

But wait! Some will protest that political strategy was not an option in New Testament times. They will say that democracy is such a new form of government that the New Testament does not speak to it. Let us explore the nature of our democracy and of our evangelical Christianity. We will see if they can be combined to operate as two parts in one strategy.

Democracy and Evangelical Christianity

Government can loosely be defined as a system of operation for a community of people. The following statements will be limited more specifically to the civil government of the United

States of America. The definition will serve to illustrate that democracy and Christianity are very different organisms. They may cooperate with great results, but they cannot be organically combined without compounding confusion for both.

Citizenship in the United States is a right of birth. Unlike Christianity, one becomes a member of the state before one understands the responsibilities of citizenship. Compulsory education in this country was established because of the recognized need to be capable of responsible citizenship. Democracy, literally meaning "the people ruling," in our country is based upon universal suffrage. That is, every individual has an equal unit of power—the vote. In contrast to the rule of a people by a sovereign God, the United States government is simply a way for people to rule themselves. God derives His power from who He is; our government derives its "just power from the consent of the governed."

When those two dynamics get switched or melded, problems begin. When, for example, a church becomes an institution where people are simply ruling themselves instead of trying to discern the dictates of God, the church loses its true identity. On the other hand, when people in a democracy only receive the dictates of government and refuse to try to improve those policies, democracy loses its true identity. The basis of the church is the recognized authority of God; the basis of democracy is the recognized authority of the people. Our government is made to vary with the people; religion is not. The philosopher Montesquieu, from whom our government borrowed the principle of the separation of powers, wrote, "it is the nature of human laws . . . to vary in proportion as the will of man changes; on the contrary, by the nature of the laws of religion, they are never to vary. Human laws appoint for some good; those of religion for the best; good may have another object because there are many kinds of good; but the best is but one; it cannot therefore change."[1]

The purposes of our civil government and of evangelical Christianity are also very different. In the Declaration of Independence, Thomas Jefferson wrote the assumption we as a nation have adopted. Government is the device by which we secure individual rights, "that among these are life, liberty, and the pursuit of happiness. That, to secure these rights, governments are instituted. . . ." The preamble to our Constitution develops these components further, directing that we as a group need to guard those individual opportunities to "form a more perfect union, establish justice, insure domestic tranquility, provide for the common defense, promote the general welfare, and secure the blessing of liberty to ourselves and our posterity." Our government is concerned with the order of the group so that the individual may prosper. That is also its function according to the New Testament (1 Timothy 2:1-2): "First of all, then, I urge that entreaties and prayers, petitions and thanksgivings, be made on behalf of all men, for kings and all who are in authority, in order that we may lead a tranquil and quiet life in all godliness and dignity." So protective order is the main function of our government. It may be said here that, historically and philosophically, one of its great vulnerabilities has been in its expansion of power, both domestically and in foreign endeavors. Democracy is strongest when not empire building. We have learned that while we cannot be isolated from the rest of the world, neither can we afford the mentality that says "conquer or be conquered." The wars involved in such expansion subtract liberty from our nation as well as the nations we would seek to control. Alexander Hamilton wrote in *American Federalist Papers*, "The violent destruction of life and property incident to war, the continual danger, will compel nations the most attached to liberty to resort for repose and security to institutions which have a tendency to destroy their civil and political rights. To be more safe, they at length become willing to run the risk of being less free."[2]

Evangelical Christianity has a good part of its purpose in expanding. The second part of the scriptural quote that affirms the difference in purpose continues in this way: "This is good and acceptable in the sight of God our Savior, who desires all men to be saved and to come to the knowledge of the truth" (1 Timothy 2:3-4). The word *evangelical* comes from the combination of the Greek prefix *eu-*, meaning "good," and the word *angelos*, "a messenger." An evangelical, then, is one whose purpose it is to bring good news. Traditionally, as bearers of good news, Christians want others to respond by believing the news and committing their lives to God. That is expansionism pure and simple. Unlike our government, however, it is expansionism by individual agreement. A basic difference between our government and evangelical Christianity is the contrast in concerns. Our government is concerned with the group, so that the individual may prosper. Christianity is concerned with the individual, so that the group may prosper. We have defined government as a system of operation for a community of people. Perhaps it would not be too farfetched to begin defining evangelical Christianity as a system of operation for an individual in a community of people.

The methods of civil government and evangelical Christianity are so different that to confuse them could be disastrous, as we saw in the Crusades, Spanish Inquisition, and the conquering of the new world. Essentially, we enlisted the government's force to ensure religious conformity. God grants Christianity only the power of influence to invite compliance. Our government concerns itself with our proper behavior; hence the threat of force is appropriate, since force can moderate behavior. But Christianity's concern is the heart, or attitude, thinking, and will of a person in such a deep realm, only faith is effective. Montesquieu said it well: "The influence of religion proceeds from its being believed; that of human laws from their being feared."[3]

The Religious Right

The religious right has many admirable qualities. The right-wing activists are zealous, and we all respect that. These are no wishy-washy, milksop boys and girls. These are firebrands! The question, though, is not, how valuable is religious zeal in religion? The question is, How valuable is religious zeal in government? More exactly, it is, Can religious zeal be valuable *to* government without being valuable *in* government?

The activists are practical (James 1:22) and sincere. They have a ring of certainty that is attractive. Their involvement is an act of integrity on their part. Yet for all those endearing qualities, they are missing a most important one: discernment. They have failed to discern the difference in the nature of a political system and the nature of Christianity. They have failed to discern the difference between established law and sacred law. They have also failed to discern the difference between acting responsibly toward certain issues (which Scripture specifically demands) and building a platform for political evangelism (which Scripture in no way recommends). It is not good to sew (cross-stitch?) the sacred onto a system governed by the people.

The biblical symbol for the Spirit is the dove (Matthew 3:16), traditionally associated with winsome qualities like grace, innocence, and purity. The national symbol for the U.S. is the bald eagle, traditionally associated with qualities like independence, strength, and majesty. Their qualities are certainly diverse and in many ways complementary. Yet in the following pages it will become evident that transferring evangelical Christianity onto our system of government would alter the structure of both and be a major mistake—no wiser than transplanting the wing of a dove onto the shoulder of an eagle.

Notes

1. Charles de Montesquieu, *The Spirit of Laws*, vol. 38, *Great Books of the Western World* (Chicago: Encyclopedia Britannica, 1952), 214-215.
2. Alexander Hamilton, *American Federalist Papers*, vol. 43, *Great Books of the Western World* (Chicago: Encyclopedia Britannica, 1952), 45.
3. Montesquieu, 215.

TWO

THINKERS OR TINKERS?

Five Myths About Religion and Politics (and Three Truths)

The Bible teaches that no one—not the humanist, not the revolutionary, not even the most prestigious evangelical—is impervious to a contaminated self. One reason why many persons think sin is to be found mostly in society—notably in political institutions, social structures, and multinational corporations— is that they no longer sufficiently probe their own lives to admit where sin is really to be found.

—Carl F.H. Henry

Evangelicals say the darndest things. When trying to produce thinkers' thoughts, we say things that sound like answers. But heard on a higher level, they are tinkers' talks. Tinkers are those who putter ineffectively while trying to mend something. They are sincere but naive. We will examine five oft-heard evangelical answers to political problems. In the process of such examination we will call upon a few of the greatest thinkers in Western civilization to give us counsel of caution. Proverbs 12:15 states, "The way of a fool is right in his own eyes, but a wise man is he who listens to counsel."

MYTH #1:
It's High Time the Majority Had Its Way in This Country

Many in the majority of this country feel their rights are being violated by the rights of the minority. When, for example, an accused criminal is released from the legal process by a technicality, people feel the majority is endangered. When homosexual couples are afforded marital status, there is anger. When Christians cannot express their faith in traditional public ways because the ACLU is slowly challenging traditional displays, we feel frustrated.

Then this tinker-talk solution is thrown down like a gauntlet, daring anyone to refute its logic. "This is a democracy," people say, "where the majority rules." The "might makes right" answer sounds like it can shore up the slow loss of privilege that the majority has had for so long. Note the words of the philosopher of our Constitution, James Madison: "Wherever the real power in a government lies, there is the danger of oppression. In our government the real power lies in the majority of the community."[1]

Our Constitution basically agrees with our evangelical view of people. Evangelicals and the framers of the Constitution would agree that all people are self-centered, acting in self-interest. The Constitution, unlike Christianity, does not even try to change human nature. The Constitution is interested only in working, by checks and balances, to keep all factions in their proper places. Our government is structured to keep any faction (see Federalist Paper Number 10), including the majority, from becoming too powerful. Our government does not believe that any power group, including the majority, will naturally refrain from lording it over other groups. So most of our freedoms come from negatives—things we cannot do—so they cannot be done to us. Thus we are sensitized to others by institutions. The legal system ensures that majority power can be dominant without being lethal.

It is strange to link evangelicals to a self-interested majority that needs to be held in check as all other factions do. After all, we evangelicals are supposed to be sensitive and caring. The Scriptures speak of serving. They say, "Do nothing from selfishness or empty conceit, but with humility of mind let each of you regard one another as more important than himself; do not merely look out for your own personal interests, but also for the interests of others" (Philippians 2:3-4). Yet where politics are concerned we have little or no evidence that evangelicals are any more sensitive to others' rights than any other interest group is. Zeal is understandable because we have this Great Commission to win the world. But for any group not able to muster moderation for themselves, the Constitution will muster it for them.

MYTH #2:
We've Got to Win the Battle Against Secular Humanism

This truism isn't mere tinker talk—it is rooted in fact. Yet the presentation of the fact is all wrong. In an effort to work up intensity, evangelicals turn to the language of war. Realizing that there is a spiritual warfare (Ephesians 6:10-18), we have transferred that concept to our earthly battle against the "secular humanists," those who hold man and not God as the measure and center of all things. The language used by evangelical alarmists conjures up images of conspiracy and attack. The residue of such war language is a tendency toward counterattack. Evangelicals feel persecuted by this menacing, hungry, secular humanist monster.

Another word of caution and counsel comes from seventeenth-century political philosopher Charles de Montesquieu: "It is a principle that every religion that is persecuted becomes itself persecuting; for as soon as by some accidental turn it arises from persecution, it attacks the religion which persecuted it; not as religion, but as tyranny."[2] While we might argue the concept of "accidental turn"—certainly it is no accident that Christianity came to be the great religion that it is—we understand the danger of which Montesquieu speaks. Evangelicals generally believe that secular humanism is a religion; religion can be defined in Paul Tillich's term of ultimate concern. Some evangelicals believe that secular humanists are persecuting us all by conspiratorial intention. In reality, the majority of secular humanists don't think of themselves as secular humanists; they are just folks going along with the program of the world. It is neither appropriate nor effective to attack "them" as people trying to destroy Christianity. In *The Decline and Fall of the Roman Empire*, historian Edward Gibbon recorded that Emperor Julian had "artfully fomented the religious war" to the end that the "Christians had forgotten the spirit of the Gospel, and the pagans had imbibed the spirit of the church."[3]

Attack language aimed at people is just, well, offensive. There is real danger in secular humanistic philosophy, but the evangelicals' appropriate response should be to speak the truth in love. The attack language, which usually results in personal attack, is counterproductive; it incites escalation in hate and smothers any witness to a world in need of "a more excellent way."

Let me take a minute to tell you a story I once heard that illustrates the point. For nearly three decades, from 1961 to 1989, the Berlin Wall was one of the most visible, despised, politically and ideologically charged boundaries on earth. It cut a city in two. Residents from East Berlin were not allowed to cross the wall to go into the West, and vice-versa. But that didn't stop some creative interchanges between the East and West Berliners. One night, things got a little out of hand and a group of rowdy East Berliners decided it would be funny to gather up trash and rotting garbage, douse it with sewage and toss it over the wall. So that's exactly what they did. The gross mixture splattered into several of the nicely manicured lawns of homeowners on the other side.

Quite frustrated, the homeowners called a meeting of those whose property had been despoiled. After much conversation, they agreed on a plan. That night, they gathered from their homes, clean blankets, fresh fruit and homemade breads. They placed them in big basket and lowered it over the wall.

The East Berliners were taken aback by what they saw. As they carefully lifted the goods from the basket they found a note. It read: "You can only give what you have."

We must remember that what we "give" to the world (our words and actions) reveals what is in our hearts.

MYTH #3:
We Ought to Go Back to the Good Old Days
When Christians Ran Things

History is not sure there were those good old days, and even if there were, it would not be an advancement to go back. History has one counsel for proceeding with Christian-led government: caution. When Gibbon wrote *The Decline and Fall of the Roman Empire*, he had insight into weaknesses occasioned by the Christian emperors. The conflict between "civil and ecclesiastical" jurisdiction complicated the operations of government. When Emperor Constantine became a Christian in the year 313, he linked what had been two distinct and separate institutions in society. Matters changed. As the church gained favor in the courts, the Christians took these favors to be their "just and inalienable rights" instead of luxuries afforded by the times.

As Constantine revealed his new faith, he earnestly exhorted his subjects to imitate him. With a veneer of moderation, he promised that all paganism could continue undisturbed. Then in a covert manner he undermined the safety of their ceremonies with legal technicalities. His sons followed his example "with more zeal and less discretion . . . every indulgence was shown to the illegal behavior of the Christians; every doubt was explained to the disadvantage of paganism."[4] The chance for the Christian emperors to become embroiled in religious controversies was consistently available and regularly indulged. Gibbon notes, for example, that Emperor Justinian often sacrificed the duty of father of his country to the role of defender of the faith.[5]

Not only emperors, but also clergy have diminished stature in religiopolitical governments. Philosopher Thomas Hobbes observed the negative correlation between political powers and religious fervor. His counsel was that we are not to be like those who "by too much grasping let go all." He saw the diminishing of religious leadership because "the pomp of them that obtained therein the principle public charges became by degrees so evident that they lost the inward reverence due to the pastoral function."[6] In other words, power and prestige corrupted what had been the formerly sacred office of pastor.

The church has suffered the subtraction of power resulting from its leaders' political ambitions. German philosopher Georg

Wilhelm Hegel wrote, "What Popes acquired in point of land and wealth and direct sovereignty, they lost in influence and consideration. . . . The Church was no longer a spiritual power, but an ecclesiastical one; and the relation which the secular world sustained to it was unspiritual, automatic, and destitute of independent insight and conviction."[7]

Yes, but what about when Christians were running America? Well, when was that? The amount of religious devotion within the hearts of our Founding Fathers is something only God knows. History, like Scripture, is open to interpretation. Atheists believe the Founding Fathers were deists or adherents of some other "God is not actively involved in the world" religion. We Christians tend to look upon every religious reference the Fathers made as their truest, deepest rudder for life. The truth probably lies somewhere in the middle. Both deism and Christianity were strong influences on the men who molded the policies of the new America.

We do know that the scenario of Christians benevolently and efficiently "running things" for America hasn't really happened in the past. We like the image, but it isn't real. Matters are more complicated than that. Dean Inge said once, "Like certain ministers of state, the Church has always done well in opposition, and badly in office." That is the sobering word of caution we should include in any romantic notion of Christians running things in the good old days.

MYTH #4:
We Can Fix Things If We Elect Christians Into Office

The game plan for more Christian influence in government includes a rather simplistic notion: the qualifications for office are predominantly spiritual ones. We know that Article Six of the Constitution states "no religious test shall ever be required as a qualification to any office or public trust under the United States." But that only applies to a government test, not an individual evaluation, right? Yes, but the deeper issue attached to the notion of "qualification" is relevant here. The Founding Fathers sensed that a person's religion should not be the major issue in being qualified. Some people are trying to change that. In fact, evangelicals face the temptation of so focusing on a candidate's faith that other qualifications seem irrelevant.

In an age of specialization we must understand the need for specific knowledge and skill as well as foundational faith. To operate effectively in our political system elected officials must have more than a general knowledge of how government works, or should work. Experience is critical in separating the real from the ideal. Experience is critical in building relationships necessary for group effort. Experience is critical in building long-lasting teams of trustworthy subordinates. Often officials are not sabotaged by their own mistakes but by the mistakes of those who surround them. So even if evangelicals can quickly master the new technology of the field—in media campaigning, targeting constituency subgroupings, etc.—being in government office is still an unknown skill to an amateur.

Before Christ, Plato attacked amateurism in government. In both *The Republic* and *The Statesman*, he held fast to the principle that one's expert capabilities constituted one's right to govern. In *The Republic* he outlined an ideal training program for philosopher rulers that began in early childhood and was not completed until the age of 50! While Plato's social vision and his training program are not those of a participatory democracy, his point should not be lost. Governing is a serious matter. Those who desire to rule need to have demonstrated competence in the field before they are thrust into responsibility for governing. Plato's pupil Aristotle said it this way: "If therefore, there is anyone superior in virtue and in the power of performing the best actions, him we ought to follow and obey, but he must have the capacity for action as well as virtue."[8]

MYTH #5:
We Don't Want to Force Our Religion, Just Express It

A thinker's thought: Institutional expression is not without force. As has been mentioned, the power of government and its various institutions is force. The power of Christianity is persuasion. Any and all activities carried on by governmental institutions can't help but convey the force linked with government authority. Any Christian activity expressed by a governmental institution insinuates force. To believe otherwise is amazingly naive.

What exactly do we mean by expression without force? Are we saying that we can water it down so much that it will not be forceful? Are we saying that prayer in school or the chaplain in Congress is there for decorative purposes only? Westerners think differently than the rest of the world. John Stuart Mill, the nineteenth-century political philosopher, wrote of this type of religious window dressing: "The demand [is] now so general in England for having the Bible taught, at the option of pupils or their parents, in the government schools. From the European point of view nothing can wear a fairer aspect or seem less open to objection on the score of religious freedom. To Asiatic eyes it is quite another thing. No Asiatic people ever believes that a government puts its paid officers and official machinery into motion unless it is bent on an object; and when bent on an object, no Asiatic believes that any government, except a feeble and contemptible one, pursues it by halves."[9] Children have Asiatic eyes, and so do most of us. We discern a purpose in any modeled behavior, then hold it in contempt if it is only half-pursued. The notion of institutional expression without force is at once attractive and repugnant. Lip service has always been good manners with little meaning. And our Lord always criticized those who were lukewarm.

There is also a feeling in the phrase "just be able to express it" that gives us the feeling that we are guarding or protecting Christianity. If we can just tinker with it by saying a general prayer in school or putting a nativity scene on the courthouse lawn, we feel we are fending off the infidels. Protection is appropriate at times, but protection is not our object in the faith—evangelism is! If for example, we are forced to leave off "in Jesus' name" at the end of our prayers in a public setting, is that not a betrayal rather than a harmless accommodation? When we reduce Christianity to something we can protect, or something we want to protect others from, we have lost all perspective of the sovereignty of God. He is in charge here, regardless of the laws. As John Locke wrote, "Christ . . . prescribed . . . no peculiar form of government . . . the Truth certainly would do well enough if she were once left to shift for herself. She is not taught by laws, nor has she any need of force to procure her entrance into the minds of men . . . if the Truth makes her entrance into the minds of men . . . if the Truth makes not her way into the understanding by her own light, she will be but the weaker for any borrowed force violence can add to her."[10] Locke was the philosopher our Founding Fathers looked to for their concept of religious toleration. His words of counsel here lead us to question how much government can protect Christian traditions without our substituting protection for Christian growth.

All Christians should voice and vote the values of our faith whenever possible, but let's drop the pretense that doing so has no force when allowed in a public setting.

And Now, Three Truths . . .

All five myths discussed above have some truth in them. That is why they are so popular and they strike such a chord within us. We wish the solutions were as simple and clear as those platitudes sound. In fact, it is not a simple matter to think our way to what really helps the Christian cause. Even with the help of Scripture to remind us of our purpose and to give us counsel on our attitudes, the issues are still complex. Einstein once said, "Politics is more difficult than physics." Amen. But we can know a few things about thinking Christianity in politics.

1. **We are called to be involved in government but not to depend upon it for solutions.** The Christian right seeks support in government. It could be irony, judgment, or God's great sense of humor that finds the conservatives now doing what they accused the liberals of doing for years—looking to government for solutions. We may get an answer, but never a solution. It is the nature of government to make matters more complicated. Government finds, as science does, that every answer raises more questions. Nevertheless, government is such an intricate part of our lives we cannot avoid it. When the evangelical cares about his neighbor in practical ways, participation at the polls must be a part of that caring. Like it or not, government has an effect on the poor and the elderly.

TWO – THINKERS OR TINKERS?   **37**

Like it or not, issues of justice and freedom for people are the business of government. If we want justice for our neighbor, we must ensure it by participation.

2. **We are called to be involved not only by implication but also by Christ directly.** When He said, "Render to Caesar the things that are Caesar's" (Matthew 22:21), He was telling us to respond to government's requests of us. Our government requests participation of all citizens, including evangelicals. So we obey Christ.

3. **Our government requests participation of all citizens and special interest groups.** And make no mistake about it, evangelical Christianity is a special interest group—for a specific reason. Our Founding Fathers envisioned a balance of power through healthy competition. They believed what would control each segment of society and advance society as a whole was the dynamic of the segments vying for dominance. If evangelicals do not participate with their perspective and power, they rob the American system. They also rob the American people of exposure to and the influence of the Christian perspective. American politics are competitive and complicated, but politics provides one of God's great ways of maturing our thinking and testing our commitment.

Notes

1. Richard Hofstadter, *American Political Tradition* (New York: Vintage, 1948), 3.

2. Charles de Montesquieu, *The Spirit of Laws*, vol. 38, Great Books of the Western World (Chicago: Encyclopedia Britannica, 1952), 211.

3. Edward Gibbon, *The Decline and Fall of the Roman Empire*, vol. 40, *Great Books*, 382.

4. Ibid., 329.

5. Gibbon, vol. 41, 148.

6. Thomas Hobbes, *Leviathan*, vol. 23, *Great Books*, 276.

7. Georg Wilhelm Friedrich Hegel, *Philosophy of History*, vol. 46, *Great Books*, 331.

8. Aristotle, *Politics*, vol. 9, *Great Books*, 529.

9. John Stuart Mill, *Representative Government*, vol. 43, *Great Books*, 438.

10. John Locke, *A Letter Concerning Toleration*, vol. 35, *Great Books*, 15.

THREE

THE STONE IN THE SNOWBALL:
The Problem With Every Government . . . Sin

*I believe in political equality. But there are two opposite reasons
for being a democrat. You may think all men so good that they
deserve a share in the government of the commonwealth, and so
wise that the commonwealth needs their advice…. On the other
hand, you may believe fallen men to be so wicked that not one of
them can be trusted with any irresponsible power over his fellows.
That I believe to be the true ground of democracy.*

—C.S. Lewis

Something in us will not let any of us govern very well.
The problem lies not in our methods or systems, but in
our hearts. The problem is the very first issue addressed
in Scripture after creation. According to the Bible, our problem
with governing stems from our resistance to being governed.
We have always liked the idea that we could, by some special
knowledge or some better device, have a system superior to the
one presently in place.

Adam and Eve, our parents and prototypes, are pictured trying
to extend their power. The thought that new knowledge would

automatically make things better has always been enticing. Our first parents believed that new knowledge would add a capacity for power. So, thinking with their desires, they reached beyond God's first plan for their lives (Genesis 3:11).

Going beyond their specified limits, however, they lost more than they gained. They lost the direct fellowship with God that came with doing His work His way, and the work itself became much more difficult to accomplish (Genesis 3:17-19).

That ambition and rebellion had an irreversible effect on our nature. Our tendency is still to reach for power. Since much of life has to do with power, the reasonable assumption is that the Christian community should have its share. It is an illusion, though, to believe that governmental power is better because a believer holds it. History shows no such correlation. The record is both sad and humorous. The Hebrews thought that if God's man would just rule them, certainly they would be governed perfectly. But the record of their kings is atrocious. Their priests and prophets were God's gifts to balance sinful leadership.

Centuries later, when Emperor Constantine was converted, many believed that there would not only be relief from persecution but righteousness in office. Yet the records show injustice toward nonbelievers and questionable actions in spite of Constantine's conversion. His successors in Christian political leadership could be seen as a comedy of heirs. Actually, no signs of perfection appeared for the first five hundred years after Constantine; then things got worse. Few medieval kings were any more inspiring because they governed as Christians in supposedly Christian nations. A few saintly ones, like French crusader King Louis IX (1214-1270) were renowned for heading righteous governments, but men like Louis were the exception. Even after the great theologian Thomas Aquinas had put forward the concept that God had delegated spiritual power to kings, Christian kings like Philip IV (1268-1314) of France used the theory to exalt his secular power over the church's ecclesiastical power. Talk about biting the hand that feeds you.

Since those years, much serious thought has been devoted to explaining the nature of God's involvement in governing the state. The political theorists began with definitions of the state that range from "it is a direct creation of God's" to "it is a simple social contract postulated by man as social animal." Yet no theory about the nature of the state, or what God's involvement in government should be, has changed the world's record of flawed government. No Christian leader, however dedicated to the faith, has been the solution to flawed government. Both theory and leader are devices, mechanical answers to a deeper problem of avoiding God's direct government.

It is tempting to swallow the notion that with time and learning, we are becoming unflawed as a governed people. Two American reformers did much to popularize this belief. They were more optimistic about man's ability to progressively approach perfection with government. Both a Christian and a humanist voiced very attractive hopes.

After World War I, pastor Walter Rauschenbusch became a most eloquent spokesman for the Social Gospel. He identified the phrase "Thy kingdom come, Thy will be done on earth as it is in heaven" as a command of God for this present age. He believed he saw a "growing perfection," and his followers were even more optimistic than he about "Christianizing the entire social order."[1] The democratic ideal was being provided a religious sanction; the perennial civil religion was blooming again. (It is interesting that many religious conservatives echo some of the ideals of these liberals gone by.) The mistake was, of course, that the social gospelers underestimated the enormity of sin. They believed "love covers a multitude of sins." It does. But sin infests the entire multitude of lovers. The Social Gospel movement could only recognize the difference between good and evil, not fix it.

Educator John Dewey believed man's problem was not sin, but ignorance. Man simply did not know his potential, said Dewey. As soon as he could investigate by experiment, whether in education or science or government, he would learn his way out of his problems. If people were repeatedly offered the way of love and justice and equality, of course they would happily take it. Selfishness and greed would fade away. Man would find his way up, head first. Yet it should be evident by now that thinking better cannot be equated with being better.

The return to reality began with theologian Reinhold Niebuhr, who better understood the true nature of man. Niebuhr stated plainly that shallow sentimental optimism was worse than useless. To recognize the "essential goodness of men without realizing how evil good men can be" was a monumental mistake, he said. His book *Moral Man and Immoral Society*, though it tends to equate morality with religion, still stands as an important rejection of politics that assume love and reason transcend sin. He recognized that we use evil to hold evil in check and that political answers could only approximate God's will in this life. He knew that power was a necessity for political action, but that there was no "ethical force strong enough to place inner checks upon the use of power if its quantity is inordinate." Therefore we dare not trust in a man's goodness, but we must react to his specific political plans. He noted America's tendency to choose "a messiah rather than a political leader committed to a specific political program."[2] Finally, he was most valuable in pointing out that, while there are absolutes in faith, the mistake of political religion is to absolutize what is relative in politics. He claimed that religion can be a great source of confusion in politics because of its tendency to take a stand as leader where it should be playing the role of prophet. Prophets were not political leaders. They questioned and corrected and influenced political leaders.[3] Niebuhr understood not only human sin but the need for prophecy in all ages.

The Sin That Limits Us

Adam and Eve's choice was not between being limited and unlimited. Their choice was to be limited by obedience to God or limited by internal evil. In their quest for wisdom and control, they had missed a very important consideration: We cannot use something without internalizing all aspects of that thing and being limited by it. The act of swallowing the "forbidden fruit" was more than literal. It meant that the evil as well as the good they reached for became a part of them. They sought to have a "knowledge of good and evil." They may have assumed that they could control it, that they could keep it at arm's length. But knowledge in the Bible and in life is relationship. When Scripture says, "Adam knew Eve, his wife, and she conceived, and bare Cain" (Genesis 4:1, KJV), the "knowing" is not mental objectivity, but intimate relationship. Just as Adam and Eve became a part of one another, so it is with our knowledge of anything. It becomes a part of us; not only its good but also its evil side are ingested in its entirety.

Science has recognized this truth. It has been the assumption of psychotherapy that simply teaching new information will not cure crippling mental problems. Our previously swallowed assumptions need to be brought out, pointed out, thought out, kicked out, and replaced. During the course of many brain surgery procedures, Dr. Wilder Penfield was able to demonstrate that memories are not just stored objective information. They are experiences that lie dormant in their entirety. In these surgeries, in which the patients remained awake, Dr. Penfield's electric probe stimulated the brain cells that recalled events. The events were not just remembered, they were relived. The patients could smell the same smells, hear the same music, experience the same emotions as in the original event.[4] The original event had affected the patient long after the patient had experienced the event. So we are made in such a way that what we use or grasp changes us and lives inside of us.

Unhappily Ever After (Each Other)

We have already discussed in chapter one the different natures of church and state, or more accurately, Christianity and civil government. Christianity is strongest when its only force is persuasion; civil government's ultimate strength is its ability to use force. Christianity was made to expand; civil government has definite weaknesses in its expansion. Christianity has its authority from above; our civil government has its authority by the consent of the governed. Such are differences in their natures at present. A further question to be considered now is this: If evangelicals reach for the political fruit as the main tool for increasing our influence, will we pay a higher price than we expect? There is a familiar saying between lovers: "I love you not only for what you are, but for what I become when I am with you." It is an affirmation that we are profoundly changed in intimate relationship. Our consumer mentality that suggests that we can use and dispose of anything without being affected does not take into account the fact that we are being constantly changed. Because of that fact, memorialized by Adam and Eve and some forbidden fruit, we must watch closely what we grasp so that we can protect our nature from further confusion. That is as true for institutions as it is for individuals.

The most dangerous aspect of politics is the thirst for power. The distinction between Christianity that operates in politics because of its civil responsibility and Christianity that longs for political power is not unlike a "dangling chad." It takes an expert eye to reveal the intent of the aspirant, but even experts, being human, can only take their best guess. Christians who enter the political arena for purposes other than service, sooner or later, will find that their intentions have not helped the Christian cause. Robert Dahl's book *Who Governs?* contrasts *homo civicus* and *homo politicus*—civic man and political man. He basically writes that civic man is a social being. He knows the quality of his life depends upon the health of the society in which he lives. He improves the environment for relationships by his activities in society, including his vote. He does not put the importance of government above duty to family, church, and friends unless the government threatens to limit freedoms he sees as important.

Political man, on the other hand, regards political involvement as a way of gratifying his needs and getting his way. He is much more in love with power than civic man. He attempts to gain control over civic man, and only when civic man perceives that threat will he take action to thwart political man. For political man, politics is a way of life, and power is the breakfast of champions. For civic man, relationships are a way of life, while politics and power are only periodic necessities.

As Christians strive to be true to the New Testament, we become highly suspicious of political man. Nowhere in the New Testament does it exhort individuals to political dominance. By contrast political power relationships are forbidden by Christ or transformed into an act of service (Matthew 20:25-28). Christendom must not ingest politics in general, or its focus and character will change drastically. Cooperation is appropriate, individual contribution is necessary to obedience, continuing conversation is a mutual duty at all times, but merging the institutions of church and state is out.

The wisdom of a fourth-grader will close the point. When the class was asked by the teacher to do some creative writing, students took out their papers. "Write a story of romance," said the teacher. Johnny was finished within a few moments. His story had three sentences: He said, "Will you marry me?" She said, "No." And they lived happily ever after.

Killer Tendencies

Many evangelicals stay away from politics. Our parents taught us that conversations about politics (and religion) could be hazardous to the health of relationships, and they had good reason. Part of politics is the art of gaining control. It is a manifestation of our sinful nature that can cause every deliberation over power to become a power struggle itself. Experience has taught us and intuition warns us that politics is volatile. It can change in an instant from helpful to hurtful, from service-oriented to dominating, from benign to malignant and back again. Politics is not just a subject, it is a positioning. The very topic has a subtle way of calling us from trust to suspicion. Even conversations that end amicably leave lingering distances if the conversants are not in perfect agreement. The ideal of pluralism—an ideal that we insist is what makes America free—becomes more frustration than goal in political conversation. The ideal of pluralism that should safeguard our relationships by not insisting on agreement before togetherness belongs to a realm of maturity that many admire but few desire. In fact, there is something hidden in opinions tossed out, like a stone in a snowball, that changes conversations from fun competition to war. If we could isolate and extract that thing, we might go far in keeping people from becoming enemies.

The danger to our peace is the amount of profit and loss. The smaller the gain of one group over the other, the more equity we have in our nation. Equity both promotes and controls competition. Gross inequity almost ensures rebellion and fanaticism. But a system in which both sides of any issue have much more to lose than that particular battle, and in which the loss of that battle will not mortally wound their cause, can thrive on competition. Each side can be kept stimulated and more attentive because of the close competition. It's been said "What doesn't kill you makes you stronger." Each side can build a life that does not depend upon, and will not be destroyed by, the outcome of the competition. Such is the ideal for which the framers of our Constitution strove. Creating a series of checks and balances that would ensure as little inequity as possible and make tyranny by any group unlikely, they gave us all a great gift. But the stone in the snowball could still ruin it. Even great and mighty giants can be felled with a stone. What is the stone hidden in other forms? And once we find it, can we extract it? And if we can extract it, will we?

The Central Problem in Individuals

The stone in the snowball is self-centeredness; ego always wants to be at the center of things. This does not sound like a surprising or difficult concept to grasp. In fact, it is so familiar that it goes without heed. It is not spiritual enough for evangelicals to address; it is not unusual enough for others to notice. Yet ego is at the heart of the matter. Let us first define the concept of ego as it is used here, and then go on to explore its destructive capabilities.

In a way, I dislike depending on a Freudian term to characterize so important a problem. As an evangelical I have this feeling that I should be able to come up with some strictly biblical term that would define such a world problem. But the very fact that I desire to twist understanding and control terms to make me and my group look good is evidence of the problem itself: ego. Samuel Taylor Coleridge once said, "He who begins by loving Christianity better than truth will proceed by loving his own sect or church better than Christianity, and end in loving himself better than all." So, while I do take comfort in knowing that the Bible's descriptions of people match and predate the term *ego*, it is still the secular term that is helpful in analyzing the problem. We need not go too deeply into psychoanalytic theory. To do so would cloud the concept. The common understanding of the term is valuable: the Ego (which I will henceforth spell with a capital *E*) is the "I" of everything. I will use capital *E* in Ego to connote the narcissistic emphasis. The Ego projects itself into the middle of every issue. The Ego determines the interest in, and understanding of, any issue. The Ego is active in protecting the individual's identity from confusion and intrusion. The Ego is not synonymous with sin; sin is more subtle and negative. The Ego is not evil. Relationships are built on the presupposition of individual identity, and sickness inhabits relationships when any of the individuals' identities are confused or diminished. A sense of relevancy is built on the relationship of an issue to an individual's identity. Again, the relationship is unhealthy when the identity is tied too closely to the issue so that either issue or identity is less than distinct. The Ego, then, is not a problem. The size of the Ego, or its proportion to the whole, can be a problem. A piece of gravel in a snowball is insignificant; a rock makes the snowball a weapon.

Destruction is inherent in political strategy when Ego concerns are the motivation for the effort. The Ego concerns are, in our popular nonclinical definition, the driving force to make ourselves the center of every effort and the standard of measure for every policy. Ego is the leaven that turns our gratitude for privileges into an arrogant attitude of entitlement. Such a transformation is recorded many times in the New Testament; it is microcosmed in Luke 18:9-14. The Pharisee is privileged with the spiritual leadership of the times, but he lets that privilege turn to arrogance. Foremost in his mind is that he ranks better than others. "I thank you that I am not like other men." His position has become in his mind such a fixed right that it does not occur to him to ask for forgiveness or correction. It is the habit of those who are privileged to turn privilege from a responsibility into a protected ranking. And it is easier for us to protect our ranking by institutionalizing it, rather than by continuing the effort that led to it. This desire to make "I" the higher standard of measure is the beginning of sin (Genesis 3:5).

Self-righteousness can be institutionalized. The first institutionalizing of self-righteousness can happen within a recognized church structure. For example, ordination, meant to be a recognition of God's particular call, can become itself substitution for a person's direct dependence on God. A pastor or bishop may lose all humility and exercise his authority without any regard for the Lord of the church. The second institutionalizing of self-righteousness can occur in the political sphere. For example, a voter can intend for his religious candidate's attainment of office to be a mandate for his religion to be the norm. That provides the believer with a false source of security, and it infects the state with a skewed sense of sovereignty. No institution can perpetuate individual righteousness, at least not from an evangelical point of view.

The Central Problem in Groups

Such Ego tendencies are every bit as characteristic of groups as they are of individuals. We would do well to recognize that we are social beings who not only magnify our individual tendencies by group but also intensify our individual evil possibilities in groups. The importance of group life is documented both in Scripture and in simple sociological observation. Since God determined that it is "not good for man to be alone" (Genesis 2:18), the effects others have on us and how we sin have been recorded. The influence of group dynamics in shaping the perceptions and actions of its constituent individuals is evident. Also, the personalities of groups themselves are important to note.

Our individual Ego concerns lead us to be a part of a group. Different kinds of groups influence our interaction with the world. But they do not necessarily diminish our Ego tendencies toward being the center of attention and the standard of measure.

One group is the *primary group*, the supreme example of which is the family. The primary group pays intense attention to us (many times reinforcing our "center of things" perspective). It molds our values and our method of operation. It is the significant source of fact and interpretation of reality. It can give us stability and security and a sense of belonging while we deal with our environment. Our interest here is rather in the groups chosen as resources for societal influence. These *secondary groups* reflect our concerns, and we use them as devices to manipulate our environment.

Most secondary groups to which we turn are of our own choosing, reflecting our own purposes. Their influence upon us may not be as personal as the primary group's. Our influence upon them is not as direct or significant. Yet we see them as our chance for our greatest societal impact. A few close friends who discuss politics make up a primary group; a political party is an example of a secondary group. Longtime neighbors who wish to protect each other from harm compose a primary group; the armed forces is a secondary group

The result of the investment in the group is a magnified reliance upon the group's importance. The group needs to be the center; the group needs to be the standard of measure. Furthermore, every group has two personalities. One relates to the world. Its objectives in relation to the world are usually published. In a political party the objective goal statement usually can be found in the party platform. The voters are to compare the platforms of two (or more) parties. The other personalities of groups relates to an inward agenda, one concerned with their constituents. There is an investment in individual selves that makes the secondary group more responsive to its constituency than to the agenda outside its constituency. The group becomes an entity that not only has an impact on behalf of its constituents but also a reward for its constituents. It becomes a means of increasing their privilege as well as a tool for their service.

The subtle effect of Ego upon a group is that the group projects its needs and values upon everyone. This tendency is even more pronounced with increased dominion. It makes the group both arrogant and ignorant when it comes to using power. Niebuhr describes this phenomenon:

> The moral attitudes of dominant and privileged groups are characterized by universal self-deception and hypocrisy . . . The reason why privileged classes are more hypocritical than underprivileged ones is that special privilege can be defended only by proving that it contributes something to the good of the whole. Since inequalities are greater than could possibly be defended rationally, the intelligence of privileged groups is usually applied to the task of inventing specious proofs for the theory that universal values spring from, and that general interests are served by, *the special privileges which they hold.*[5]

Notice that it is not the group's truth that is being defended, but the group's privilege or position. That is Ego.

When the focus of a group is upon self, the inevitable conflict with other "self groups" produces less than moral behavior. Dr. M. Scott Peck, in analyzing the subject of group evil at the My Lai massacre, shares this observation: "For many years it has seemed to me that human groups tend to behave in much the same ways as human individuals—except at a level that is more primitive and immature than one might expect. Why this is so—why the behavior of groups is strikingly immature—why they are, from a psychological standpoint, less than the sum of their parts—is a question beyond my capacity to answer."[6] Nazi government in Germany began as a source of pride for the German people after their defeat in World War I. It restored to them the esteem that comes with group Ego. But in the conflict of World War II, the extermination of 6 million Jews was a result of Ego rationalization turned into evil destruction.

A Delicate Surgery

The question arises whether it is possible to separate personal participation in a group from selfish ambition by a group. There must be some treatment, perhaps an extraction, that can prevent self-destruction by group success. There is such a treatment. It involves early detection, relentless limitation, and radiating faith.

The signs of worth and pride are often the same. For example, these days many cars' bumpers extol the virtues of the church named, "_____: the church that cares." Some churches advertise a more perfect example of the point: a pun. One read, "Life begins at Calvary." Calvary is, of course, not only the place of the cross but also the name of the church. Some churches, whose names include the word *First* because of chronological foundation, advertise their congregations as "The First Family." It could be that all of these churches simply and sincerely are doing the best they know to invite folks to their churches so that the folks can meet the Lord. But any church can easily slip into self-centeredness, where displaying the bumper sticker is a matter of pride and positioning. (I have never seen a bumper sticker that humbly stated, "_____: just one of God's churches.") In any institution it is difficult to tell where reasonable self-esteem turns into self-centeredness. But that does not mean we should not try to detect such a transformation. Probably the best scriptural instrument for differentiating healthy self-esteem from self-centeredness is found in 1 Corinthians 13:4-7. Genuine love is the antithesis of self-centeredness. The qualities of love can be used as a checklist of attitudes, so that the transformation of Ego can be detected. When asked in the form of questions applied to opposing people or groups, the qualities provide a standard of insight. Am I patient with them? Am I kind when I talk of them? Do I envy them? Do I vaunt myself (or my group or my cause) over them instead of uplifting them as people? Am I seeking them or desiring to see myself in them? Original sin begins again every time our own power becomes our focus and our own increase is a delight to our eyes. Original sin proceeds every time we accept a voice that confirms that focus. Our group can easily supplant the serpent.

In this context the phrase "relentless limitation" refers to purity of motive. The words of Colossians 3:23 are as true in our participation in the political realm as in anything else, "Whatever you do, do your work heartily, as for the Lord rather than for men." It is, indeed, tempting to work for men—ourselves, or our group—rather than for the Lord. The relentless limitation that is so necessary is limitation on our imperialism—the spread of ourselves as the center of things. We want to make others a part of our agenda rather than offer to become a part of their lives. When Christ spoke to his disciples about greatness (Matthew 20:20-28; Mark 9:33-35; Luke 22:24-27), He did not censure their desire for influence, but He limited their attitude of imperialism.

THREE - THE STONE IN THE SNOWBALL

They were not to "lord over" people, they were to be at people's service, as He had been.

How can we, as groups or individuals, limit ourselves in intention but not activity? Consistent spiritual self-examination can alert us to a spreading disease. Some commonsense questions will help. What do we know of the people we intend to serve, especially the opposition, from their own mouths? How can we walk among them? What can they teach us? When Peter tells Christians to "honor all men" (1 Peter 2:17), that is a relentless necessity.

Separation of Sin and State

If the Ego begins as the tendency toward self-centered immaturity, then the last step of Ego unchecked is an effort toward dominance. The desire of the Ego is not for cooperation (which is complicated, and which requires time and effort), but for control over our lives and over others' lives. The result is to reach for devices that will allow us to dominate. The most overt device of dominance is political power: the government. How we relate to the government will determine whether we are using it as an expression of our individual but neighborly values, as a platform for our own self-centeredness, or as a weapon for our dominance. Separation of self and government is not productive, but as believers we must separate ourselves from the use of the government for dominance. How can we relate to political power in a way that will allow us to express our individuality without giving into the sin of attempted political domination?

Evangelical Christians have a chance to model self-imposed limitations. Ideological combat in this world is seldom possible (or wise) to avoid. Christians have a distinct worldview that has its basis in a purpose beyond this world. The people in the world and of the world will not agree on this basis, so there will be conflict (John 16:33). The conflict is legitimate. In a world where people search for meaning, and their answers to that search vary; disagreements are inevitable. The conflicts can be opportunities to witness and to model restraint in the use of power.

Christians in ideological conflict with the world can model what the world has seldom seen—persons placing a limit on how much power they will stockpile. The world needs this kind of disciplined witness.

Notes

1. Walter Rauschenbusch, *A Theology for the Social Gospel* (New York: Macmillan, 1917), 142.
2. "The National Election," *Radical Religion*, Winter 1936, 142.
3. Arthur Schlesinger, Jr., "Reinhold Niebuhr's Role in Political Thought," in *Reinhold Niebuhr: His Religious, Social, and Political Thought*, ed. Charles Kegley and Robert Bretall (New York: Macmillan, 1956), 149.
4. W. Penfield, "Memory Mechanisms," *AMA Archives of Neurology and Psychiatry*, vol. 67 (1952), 178-198.
5. Reinhold Niebuhr, *Moral Man and Immoral Society* (New York: Scribner's, 1932), 117.
6. M. Scott Peck, *People of the Lie* (New York: Simon and Schuster, 1983), 216.

FOUR

THE RIGHTEOUS AMERICAN GROUP:
How Thinking Christians React to an Imperfect Government

Liberty without obedience is confusion, and obedience without liberty is slavery. —William Penn

The opening chapters of this book emphasized caution about Christian politics. Its theme was that we should not swallow the simplistic myth that we have done our duty if we elect godly people to high office. But if we can have an electorate of godly people doing their duty, the government will reflect more godly principles naturally. Our job is not to convert the government, our job is to be personally transformed into the image of Christ. The Bible is not as concerned with how religious a government is; rather the concern is how righteous the people are, including how righteously they respond to their government. The *people* are the objective.

The first step in understanding this principle comes with a reread of the Scriptures, keeping a God-government theme in mind. We are like the congregation member who was asked to lead a worship service. Although he had been sitting through the same worship format for years, he came the next Sunday with a notepad. He explained, "I once came to receive leadership in my worship experience. If am going to be called to give leadership, I need to look at the same thing with a new perspective." If we common folk are going to be called to full participation and leadership, we need to take a look at the Scriptures from a different vantage point.

The Importance and Unimportance of Structure

Though the Old Testament and New Testament are quite different in presenting the way God leads His people, the intention of God is always the same. He desires to be our God and desires us to be His people (Isaiah 43:21). That desire may be accomplished through different forms of government, but not through anarchy (Jude 5-8). God will use some form of government to provide an environment in which we may come to Him. God has used different forms of governments and has worked His purpose in each (Daniel 2:21). Yet the human governments themselves are limited in their importance to God (Isaiah 40:15, 17, 23-25), because He is sovereign in their existence (Isaiah 41:2-4).

The forms He used in the Old Testament period varied much more than the civil government forms used in the New Testament. A quick overview of history can highlight the changes in governmental form. When God called forth a people to be under His direct leadership (Genesis 12:1-3), the patriarchal structure of the family sufficed for government. No special anointing for leadership was mentioned, no elaboration of structure was given. A son of the patriarchal government, Joseph, found himself a leader in another type of civil government, and God used that pagan government to accomplish His purpose (Genesis 50:20). Just as God used Joseph, a believer in a nonbelievers' government, later He used Moses, a believer, *against* that government. With Moses we see that God called His people to another form of government, with His appointed leader and purpose. He does direct Moses, eventually, to rely upon a more elaborate structure with the Law (Exodus 20), the priesthood (Exodus 19:22), and the court system (Deuteronomy 1:12-17). Then during the period of the judges we see God raise up temporary leaders, effective in short-term government but made ineffectual in the long run by the peoples' unrighteousness. In hindsight, we see the general spiritual principle of government written in Proverbs 14:34: "Righteousness exalts a nation, but sin is a disgrace to any people." Later, despite God's warning, Israel demands a king (1 Samuel 8) as a substitute for God's direct kingship over their lives. God anoints Kings Saul, David, and Solomon to unite the kingdom, and also raises up prophets like Nathan to confront perversions in government (2 Samuel 12:1-14). During the ensuing period of the divided kingdom and corrupt kings, God continues to use the voice of prophets to correct or confront government. Following that period, God even used captivity by a foreign government (2 Kings 15:29; 17:6) as part of His government of Israel. Foreign kings became His instruments (Isaiah 45:1) and Israel learns the cost of inattentiveness. After the Babylonian captivity, Israel returns to a civil government dominated by various foreign powers, except for a brief period under the Maccabees (Jewish leaders who rededicated the temple). The last dominant power noted in Scripture is the Roman Empire.

It is during the post-exilic period that separation of religion and state becomes a necessity for ongoing life. Spiritual authority is only loosely connected with government. The Jews and, later, Christians are too devoted to their faith to look to the state for the ultimate leadership in their lives. During Christ's time, Rome delegated certain religious and civil authority to the Sanhedrin, the Jewish ruling council. During this period provincial civil rulers, like Pontius Pilate, had ultimate but tenuous authority. To keep the peace and, therefore, his job, the provincial ruler had to pay attention to the independence-minded Jewish religious leaders. In time, however, the Jews had no religious input into civil government. Jerusalem was destroyed in A.D. 70, and the civil government both completely dominated and periodically persecuted the Christians.

God, we believe, moves in mysterious ways. We even believe that He was working in the various forms of government. He does not depend on one standard form of government to achieve His ends.

Biblical Principles and Civil Governments

We should be released from a nagging suspicion that if we just got the form of government right the Spirit would be able to work. In the different forms of government the Spirit is constantly at work, bringing God's people to Him. However, God is recorded as alternately working through, in spite of, or against certain governments. Though God uses all governments for His ultimate purpose, He does not react the same toward all governments — and neither will the people who follow Him.

There are at least five reactions to civil governments given in Scripture.

1. *Obedience*. Obedience is the primary reaction in Scripture. Our God is a God of order. To eliminate chaos He has put certain structures into our lives. They reflect His nature and our need for

order. They also test whether we can learn the most valuable trait in following God—submission. If we cannot submit to what we have seen, how can we submit to what we have not seen? For these reasons Romans 13:1-2 states, "Let every person be in subjection to the governing authorities. For there is no authority except from God, and God establishes those that exist. Therefore he who resists authority has opposed the ordinance of God." Notice the connection between civil and spiritual submission. Governments teach us something that has spiritual significance: we cannot always have our own way. Our reaction to earthly authority certainly indicates our reaction to heavenly authority. If we respond positively to authority, it means we recognize the necessity of structure. The structure of civil government keeps us safe from each other and foreign threats. Paul, in 1 Timothy 2:1-2, requests prayer for governing authorities "in order that we may lead a tranquil and quiet life." With our basic need for security met, we are free to turn our attention and energies toward the meaning of life.

Civil government is just one of the structures of the universe necessary for accumulating meaningful purpose. A strong marriage will permit freedom and development in the individual partners. A strong sense of parental stability gives a child the foundation needed to explore the world. Secure employment gives the employee the ability to focus on family, friends, and ministry. Just as the structure in music frees the notes to vary and create beauty, so the stronger structures in our lives allow us freedom to be creative. Maintenance of the structures of life is a minimal investment of time for the return of security and stability they give. Christians in politics are our investment in maintaining the structure of civil government. Christians obeying that structure of government are paying the minimal daily requirement for getting on with the real substance of life.

2. *Repentance*. Repentance can be an appropriate reaction to government. If God's concern is the nearness of His people to Him, He may allow disruptions in the structures of society (including government) as a sign to repent. In 2 Chronicles 7:13-14, God plainly states, "If I send pestilence among My people, and My people who are called by My name humble themselves and pray, and seek My face and turn from their wicked ways, then I will hear from heaven, will forgive their sin, and will heal their land." Christians, then, can use even the worst forms of government as a cause for self-examination and spiritual growth. Too often our reflex is to try to fix the pestilence before we fix ourselves. An excellent question to ask ourselves whenever we recognize government's inadequacy is, "How can I use this 'pestilence' to help me depend upon God rather than government and change my life for the better?" All forms of government should spur us to godly behavior (Romans 13:3-5) so that God's will may "be done on earth as it is in heaven." A Christian involved in politics should have personal repentance rather than governmental reform as a primary agenda.

3. *Civil Disobedience*. We must also recognize there are times when civil disobedience is the appropriate reaction to a governmental edict. The obvious example is Acts 4:18-20, when believers were ordered to do what was directly opposed to what they knew to be right. "And when they had summoned them [the apostles], they commanded them not to speak or teach at all in the name of Jesus. But Peter and John answered and said to them,

'Whether it is right in the sight of God to give heed to you rather than to God, you be the judge; for we cannot stop speaking what we have seen and heard.' " The same dynamic is reported in Acts 5:29 where the apostles state flatly, "We must obey God rather than men." Civil disobedience was Daniel's witness also. The important aspect of biblical civil disobedience is its *motivation*. It is done when there is a direct conflict between what the government would force an individual to do and what God would have him do. It is not an attempt at government reform so much as it is a personal moral necessity. It is not a matter of having one's rights violated; it is a matter of being forced to do what is wrong. Therefore, though Scripture validates civil disobedience, it does not see it as primarily a political tool. Rather, civil disobedience is a last stand against a perverted government, a stand that includes accepting the punishment. A good question to screen an act of civil disobedience is, "Is this disobedience a witness against a government action that forces me and others to do wrong, or is it simply a strategy to gain political power?" In the first instance, one is obeying a greater structure of the universe—moral law. In the second instance, one may be putting self above obeying God-given structure, and that is not a Christian's option.

4. *Correction*. Correction (not rebellion) is a biblical response to government. In the Old Testament there are many instances where God sent a prophet to challenge the direction of a government (1 Kings 12:21-24, for example). In the New Testament, John the Baptist tried to correct Herod (Matthew 14:4) and was killed because of it. Yet not all corrections of government took the form of confrontations. Esther and Joseph were two believers who became a part of the government personnel and had a profound

effect on policy. Their participation in government made a distinct difference in the civil government's attitude toward God's people. Paul progressed through the Roman judicial system (Acts 25:11) with a goal of influencing people for Christ as he went (Acts 26:27-29). His goal was to make a difference in the lives of political officeholders. Paul, like other biblical figures, was someone who could have been an enemy of the government, but instead was a friend who offered a correction in course. Scripture pictures reproof as a part of love (Proverbs 3:12) and as a real help to the wise (Proverbs 9:8; 10:17; 12:1; 13:18; 15:5).

Americans are both blessed and challenged by living under a political system that is designed for ongoing correction in its development. Our Constitution is a developing document. It will be interpreted and amended over the years according to the character of the nation. Our democracy depends upon correction as circumstances change. Unlike a totalitarian system that must defend itself against change, democracy theoretically calls for mid-course correction via input from the people. So the reaction of correction is not only modeled in Scripture, it is necessary in our system of government.

5. *Transplanting.* Transplanting is another scriptural reaction to government, and it is the most complicated. When a Christian is living under a government that he finds most ungodly, he may find that neither civil disobedience nor correction is an appropriate option. A logical choice is rebellion, but rebellion is not a scriptural option. There is simply no way to reconcile the concepts of rebellion and submission to the governing authorities. Rebellion is a form of anarchy, which is the complete absence of government and law. Anarchy is a condition where each individual goes his own way and

chaos reigns. It violates the structure of the universe and the nature of God. God holds anarchy in such abhorrence that His servant, Joshua, advises people to serve false gods rather than no God: "If it is disagreeable in your sight to serve the Lord, choose for yourselves today whom you will serve: whether the gods which your fathers served which were beyond the River, or the gods of the Amorites in whose land you are living; but as for me and my house, we will serve the Lord" (Joshua 24:15). Anarchy exalts the individual to the status of a god and precludes any form of submission except that which comes from human whim.

The first (and sometimes last) step toward anarchy is rebellion. Rebellion is the nonsubmission to authority while pretending to live under that authority. Rebellion is the individual raising himself above the government or placing himself outside the law. Rebellion is not *for*, it is *against*. It is purely negative, and there is no kind word for it in Scripture. What, then, is a scriptural answer for those who feel compelled to be against an evil government? They must be against the evil government from without, not from within. If attempting open correction is not an option, and civil disobedience is not necessary, then the believer must be transplanted to be submissive to a different authority.

In Matthew 2:13, we read of an evil government that demands the life of the infant Jesus. Neither correction nor civil disobedience was an appropriate reaction to that government. So "an angel of the Lord appeared to Joseph in a dream, saying, 'Arise and take the Child and His mother, and flee to Egypt, and remain there until I tell you; for Herod is going to search for the Child to destroy Him.' " In this case Joseph, Mary, and the child were transplanted under a civil government that took no issue with the government from which they had come; the

agenda was simply safety. A like circumstance is described in
Matthew 10:23, where Jesus is instructing His disciples, "But
whenever they persecute you in this city, flee to the next." The act
of transplanting from one set of city fathers to the next is not one
of government reform, it is a strategy for safety and continuing
ministry. The respect for and submission to a civil government
is still a part of the individual's life, but, in an effort to continue
his life and ministry, he leaves the country. This biblical strategy
would work toward the ideal that any person ought to be able to
leave a country for the purposes of life or ministry.

Our own American Revolution looked like pure rebellion,
but it was actually the birth of a new nation. The Declaration of
Independence clearly separated the people from English authority.
The Constitution completed that separation by instituting a
legitimate civil government. After attempted correction, the
next step was transplantation by creation of a new governmental
authority. Because of the geographic separation, the colonies
were already predisposed toward self-government. In many
ways the American people had already begun to form an identity
and government separate from Britain. The "taxation without
representation" issue was more an evidence of a separate ethos
and people than of subjects who wanted more involvement in
British government.

Each of these reactions is rooted in respect for, and the need
for, authority. No matter what the form of government, Christians
are called to recognize the necessity of government.

A Centering Scriptural Principle

One concept in the Bible is critical in determining appropriate
action for Christians in many arenas, including politics. The

concept has not been used much in a practical way because it has not been understood completely by the general Christian populace. When most Christians are asked about scriptural guidelines for Christian involvement in government, we make a beeline to a Bible concordance or a topical index. We proceed to look up *government* or *authority* or *citizenship*. We then attempt to tie the pack of principles we have found into some semblance of order. We sense the need for an overarching principle to help us interpret and order the various passages, but we can't seem to pull one out of the pack. Well, there is such a principle. It is just not in "the pack." *The principle is the biblical concept of righteousness.* The mere mention of the term *righteousness* may cause some of us to do some holy head-nodding or to look with enthusiastic anticipation toward our next opportunity for lambasting the evils of society. Such reflexes show how misunderstood the concept is. Righteousness is actually a practical concept, helpful in everyday ways. Let us first define it accurately, and then apply it to Christians in politics.

The best definition of righteousness I have ever read was also the simplest. Doctors Elizabeth and Paul Achtemeier, Old and New Testament scholars respectively, sum up the scriptural definition of righteousness in this way: "The fulfillment of the demands of a relationship, whether with men or with God."[1] If we look up different passages containing the word *righteousness* in the Bible, we will not only see that this is an accurate definition, but it also points to practical application.

It is strange that the concept of righteousness is so often used in the Bible and so seldom used by us. Part of our clumsiness in handling this important concept is our confusion as to what it really means. Many of us have assumed righteousness to be a synonym for holiness, or goodness, or moralism. In fact, it is quite different than each of these. Holiness implies a separation, a withdrawal from common use; righteousness implies not separation but linking in relationship. Goodness has a Hebrew root meaning of "pleasant." It is a positive, beneficent term, but not specific. Righteousness, on the other hand, only works in specifics. Moralism is the offensive twin of goodness. Goodness intimates; moralism intimidates. Moralism commands behavior in universal absolutes; it is the answer waiting in ambush for a question. Righteousness, however, arises from relationships where persons as well as questions are addressed, and respect as well as an answer is given. And to clarify, that differs from relativism since righteousness always has God in mind when responding to people.

It may surprise many to know that biblical righteousness is not a matter of universal standards but of particular relationship. The Old Testament is consistent with the New Testament: the context of righteousness is a specific relationship. When Abraham "believed in the Lord; and He reckoned it to him as righteousness" (Genesis 15:6), we see the forming of a specific relationship. Faith, neither performance nor obeying the rules of the universe, was what brought Abraham into relationship with a personal God. Faith was what God wanted. According to Paul's writing in Galatians, Christ was sent to relieve us of a bondage to some cold, universal standard of behavior (what the Law had become) and restore us to a trusting relationship with God. The relationship fulfills God's nature of love: "We love, because He first loved us" (1 John 4:19). The relevant point here is that when our God-given government asks us to do something, we respond to that demand because we have a relationship with our government. And when we do respond by being politically active, any righteous action will benefit others and not just ourselves. Jesus summarized the foundation for the law not in terms of obedience, but in terms of love (Matthew 22:36-40).

The biblical principle of righteousness requires us to fulfill the demands of each relationship as is appropriate. The relationship need not have an explicit religious purpose to be the context for righteousness. The attentive father or mother, the conscientious worker, the servant leader, the helpful friend, the loving spouse, and the voting citizen are all being righteous in these areas. While moral absolutes exist, the Christlike love in relationships is the point of righteousness. Universal standards for behavior in all relationships exist, but righteousness begins with an appropriate behavior in a particular relationship. As Proverbs 15:28 says, "The heart of the righteous ponders how to answer." Righteousness thrives in relationships where demands are clarified, agreed upon, and binding. When we find and keep valid demands in a relationship, we fulfill the righteousness God has imputed to us in Christ.

Our Responsibility to Relate

Among our many relationships is the one with our government. All Christians have a responsibility to relate to the government that has authority over them (Romans 13:1-7). United States citizens are bound in a unique and positive way to a special form of government.

There are several reasons why Christians are reluctant to take an active place in steering our government. Some people believe that civil government deals with worldly issues and such issues are not the Christian's concern. They believe that the kingdom of

God is the antithesis of the evil world and, therefore, they should separate themselves from such worldly concerns. In a sense, many are like our brothers and sisters in the Amish tradition. Stick with the horse and buggy, because once you start involvement with the things of the world, it is difficult to draw the line.

Some other Christians just have no interest whatsoever in political issues. They are very glad to take the passenger's seat. Wherever they are driven, within reason, is fine with them. They just have no attraction toward that steering wheel.

Others could have an interest, but the additional demands of life are overwhelming. They just do not have the time to consider one more thing—especially something as huge as politics. They would say, "You drive, because I have four things I need to get done between here and wherever we are going."

Some people have never seriously considered politics before and are afraid to start now. They believe that the issues are too complex to ever understand. Or they may be so cynical about politics that they won't participate "because it doesn't make any difference." There are dozens of understandable reasons why people avoid responsible involvement in our political process. There are also a few bad reasons, one being laziness. But there are no righteous reasons for not taking some responsibility in our government, because our government demands that we participate as our part of the relationship.

We owe our government. When Jesus said, "Then render to Caesar the things that are Caesar's; and to God the things that are God's," He was giving more than one-time advice. He was stating the principle of righteousness. We are to pay what the government demands, not just in taxes, but also in participation. Inasmuch as we threw patriotism out the window in the 1960s because of some valid concerns about the Vietnam War, we threw the proverbial baby out with the bathwater. There is a place in the Bible for giving to the government what is due because God can work in us and in government through that involvement. What, then, does the United States government demand of us?

Loyalty. In gleaning concepts from our most important government documents, the Declaration of Independence and the Constitution, we may note at least four demands our government makes of us. The first demand is one of *loyalty.* The last sentence of the Declaration of Independence announces both a reliance upon God and an attachment to each other as requirements for continued freedom: "And, for the support of this declaration, with a firm reliance on the protection of Divine Providence, we mutually pledge to each other our lives, our fortunes, and our sacred honour." The mutual pledge to each other is more than a nice promise. It gives us more than security. Indeed, our loyalty to this nation and its government is necessary for the country's continued existence. It is the task of every government to enlist the support of the majority of its people. That consistent support, or loyalty, is what makes government a legitimate agent of the people instead of a coercive force on the people. The very nature of a democracy presupposes both genuine interest and faithfulness on the part of its people. The loyalty does not mean being a yes-man to every government policy. Quite the contrary, democracy depends upon loyalty beyond whatever answer or comment we have. Agreement is not necessary, but fidelity is. No government can be considered stable, much less effective, without the willing allegiance of its citizens. Our democracy can only be strong if we fulfill the demand of staying true to it as contrasted to any other

worldly government or no worldly government at all. As long as
we live as United States citizens, we owe this government our
loyalty as part of righteousness.

Tolerance. The second thing our government requires is
tolerance. Again, in the Declaration of Independence we read,
"All men are created equal; that they are endowed by their
Creator with certain unalienable rights; that among these are
life, liberty, and the pursuit of happiness. That, to secure these
rights, governments are instituted among men." These enduring
words of wisdom do not mention tolerance, but tolerance is the
summary of them. If all men are created equal, does not another's
opinion have as much place as mine? Truth is not a requirement
for a hearing in a democracy. Practically every reader will agree
with this general concept.

Americans value differences and are quite proud of the fact
that all people are free to hold their own beliefs. Yet experience
tells us that trouble occurs when general fundamental values are
translated into specific legislation or concrete action. We like the
ideal of tolerance, but we dislike having to actually use tolerance.
Tolerance is morally compromising within a religion, but is a
mark of maturity and civility within a country.

Tolerance is a demand from our government from two
perspectives. Our system of government will not work without
the minority possessing equal rights. The majority must prevail,
but it must be a reasoned and reasonable prevailing. Without the
protection of the law, the majority could oppress the minority.
Oppression, it should be remembered, is no more admirable when
it comes from a majority than it is when it comes from a despot.
Tolerance is the heart of the minority's reasonable protection.

Without a basic attitude of tolerance, laws and courts can drift from the democratic ideal. Additionally, the very integrity of political activism itself depends on a basic atmosphere of tolerance. One reason why relatively few Americans are politically active is their fear of conflict and rejection. Many see political disagreement as a form of violence they would be glad to avoid. An atmosphere of tolerance, emanating from people dedicated to understanding and reconciliation, is a prerequisite for most Americans' involvement. The democratic ideal envisions people who can and do disagree but are reasonable in their expression of that disagreement and respectful of their adversaries.

Understanding. The third demand our government makes on us is that of *understanding* the issues. Democracy requires understanding if citizens are to be good rulers as well as subjects. In contrast to some political systems that require only submission on the part of their subjects, democracy calls for leadership on the part of its citizens. The leadership may come through representatives elected, political action coalitions, individual influence, or a combination of all these and more. The theory, though, is clear about the objective: the people will rule. Again, the words of the Declaration of Independence speak of governments "deriving their just powers from the consent of the governed." Even as government derives its just powers from citizens, citizens derive their powers of justice from understanding. None of us can pretend to fulfill the role of citizen ruler without understanding. When our system of government calls upon us for involvement, it assumes that in our involvement we will make reasoned choices from among many alternatives for the public good. That assumption, which underlies all democratic theory, raises several significant questions:

- Am I making my choice on someone's recommendation, or do I understand the issue myself?
- Am I taking on my role as ruler (voter) on the basis of emotion or a well-thought-out decision?
- How many alternatives have I considered?
- Why is the other side for the other side?
- What is the public good in this case as differentiated from my own good or my group's good?

Involvement. The fourth demand that our government theoretically places upon us is one of *action* or *involvement.* The preamble to the Constitution of the United States of America states very clearly, "We the people of the United States ... do ..." Our government was established by the people and depends upon the involvement of the people. Yet more voters turn out on election day in totalitarian than in democratic countries, and in no other major democratic nation is participation at the polls so poor as in the United States.[2] Isn't it interesting that those who have the most power exercise it least, and that the elections in which we could have the most direct role (local elections), we are involved least of all? There are many reasons why this is so; some have been listed, others need to be discovered. The point we must stick to here, however, is that a participatory democracy presumes involvement of the people it serves. They play a crucial role in making policy and in holding the government responsible for its actions. Their participation will not only guide government but also limit it. It is the involvement of the people that ensures the healthy competition so necessary to balance and choice. Without involvement by all, power accumulates in too concentrated a form, in too few hands, in too narrow a perspective. Opposition is not a hindrance to progress; it is necessary to progress. It refines and purifies. It offers correctives. It promises problems in the future if we don't build relationships today. The ideal of involvement ensures that neither the single-issue impassioned person nor the every-issue addict will dominate the system. Democracy calls for the people who are neither extremely interested nor dogmatically decided to come into the arena, if only periodically. Otherwise we have, by default, government by political aristocracy or oligarchy.

Two Philosophies — One Course

Another simple factor in determining our social responsibility lies in deciding that it is as much our calling to be involved as it is our representative's. "All of this is ideally true," someone may say, "but there is a big difference in the way American democracy is supposed to work and the way it actually works. I've never been involved, except for voting when I can, and the country seems to be doing fine. Maybe it works better when there are only a few involved. Let us be practical. If it's not radically broken, I'm not going to spend time trying to fix it. Now what do you say to that?"

That is a perfectly understandable line of thinking. Perhaps the needs of our government are in reality quite a bit less than the ideals it puts forth. In fact, if every voter were loyal to the point of being informed and involved, would that not overload the system?

The proposition that our democracy works best when most of the voting public remains apathetic has some merit. It is recognized by most political scientists that the qualities needed to operate a democratic system smoothly are not as likely found in the average voter as in those who love politics. The average voter, it is argued, is much more likely to see his political involvement as a crusade to win benefits for himself, rather than being open to what is best for society. The average voter seems less likely to see compromise as a valuable option for progress, to recognize that government needs constant input, and to value the variety of others' opinions. The case for the average voter to remain uninvolved also assumes that our political situation is much too complicated for most to understand, therefore the pressure for simplistic solutions would increase with his involvement. In other words, the argument is that the average voter is not well-informed about the democratic principles necessary for efficient government functioning. The argument further presumes that those political people who are naturally attracted to become very involved have all of the qualities that the average voter is missing. The conclusion, then, is that the natural entropy toward of apathy has worked to everyone's benefit.

There is, of course, as strong an argument on the other side of this issue. It would propose that the average voter does have the intelligence to understand the complexity of most issues, does possess the practicality to operate within the system as it is, and does have the capacity to see beyond his own cause. The argument could go on indefinitely. The point here is not which case is stronger. The point here is one that Christians constantly face: Do we try to bring ideals down to reality, or do we try to bring reality up to the ideal?

The demands of American democracy remain the same whether the average citizen meets them or not. If righteousness fulfills the demands of the relationship, the preceding arguments are unimportant. The question is, Am I going to try to fulfill those demands of loyalty, tolerance, understanding, and involvement or not? Democracy, like Christianity, was never meant to be just an ideal—it was meant to be a norm. The question cannot be confined to how well the system is working. The concern must be broadened and deepened to what difference it makes in the lives of the individuals. Yes, the ideal is impossible to fully accomplish—that is what makes it an ideal. Each citizen will not stay informed, involved, or tolerant. Perhaps some will not even remain loyal. Yet making perfect citizens is not the Christian's agenda. Our agenda is making the God-given government's demand of every citizen normative in our own lives.

Notes

1. P.I. Achtemeier, "Righteousness in the Old Testament," *The Interpreter's Dictionary of the Bible*, vol. 4 (Nashville: Abingdon, 1962), 80, 91.

2. John Livingston and Robert Thompson, *The Consent of the Governed* (New York: Macmillan, 1966), 295.

FIVE

WHAT ARE WE *FOR*?

Issues Christians Should Care About

*The stakes are much too high for government to be a spectator
sport.*   —Barbara Jordan

We need to reverse the established trends of the religious right to attack opponents. Even well-respected and usually thoughtful leaders of the religious right vilify other Christians when they disagree with them, without first getting their facts straight. We have adopted the methods of talk radio and cross-fire TV, and diminished the art of debate so that we are fighting only *our* version of their side.

For example, in a May 2006 radio broadcast, a nationally known Christian leader mischaracterized and misquoted a well-respected evangelical leader about global warming. Richard Cizik, the Vice President of the National Association of Evangelicals (a 30-million member organization) was attacked for his stance ... only it wasn't his stance. The Christian leader quoted Richard as saying things that none of us (including Richard) would ever agree with, including, "global warming is the most important social issue of our day"; "those who are skeptical of global warming are immoral"; "he and his associates want to roll back the use of fossil fuels, oil, to the 1998 levels or even earlier, which would paralyze industry and put millions of people out of work … the net effect is anti-capitalistic and an underlying hatred for America."

Wow! Does that sound like what any of us would be for? Putting concern about global warming above the sanctity of life instead of being another expression of it? Putting millions of people out of work? Hating America? What? No!

I use this example not only because I was one of the original signers of the Evangelical Climate Initiative along with Richard (and therefore know what we are recommending and what we are not), but because this kind of rebuttal is such a clear example of what so many debaters are doing in the media: radicalizing someone's position so that they can knock it down more easily. The leader did not contact Richard to verify his facts, and then he accused Richard and his associates of trying to divide evangelicals.

I do not attribute malicious intent to this individual. He just got some wrong information and believed it. The point is that a harmful habit has crept into the way the religious right approaches points of disagreement.

So what should we do? We need to debate *ideas* accurately and respectfully!

Global warming is certainly a complex issue. Those who do not believe it is happening, or that humans do not contribute to it and can't fix it, or that there are no impending dangers connected with it, believe that because there is some evidence to support their argument. Those who do believe that global warming is real, that humans can be helpful in addressing the problem, and that it might well have some effects that are not gradual but currently volatile, also have evidence. Let's encourage the debate!

But first let me ask, is a debate a prerequisite to doing everything we can to be good stewards of creation? Do we really need to settle the scientific debate before we stop accepting pollution as a necessary evil and diligently work to devise better forms of energy usage? The issue to evangelical Christians isn't global warming; the issue is whether or not we will exercise a moral and biblical obedience to a direct command of God (Genesis 2:15). How we do that, personally and policy-wise, is something we can all work on together. We just need to keep working on it together, and that will require seeing our differences as informing instead of inflaming.

Expand the Issues and Emphasis

Conservative Christians need to be more ambidextrous rather than just "Right" or "Left" oriented. The Bible is more wholistic, more fulfilling to all of life's needs rather than heavy-handed on what is morally right or compassionately left. We need to expand our repertoire. Before we expand, though, let's sing some praises for the foundation that has been laid.

The issues that have defined evangelical voters up to this time are biblical and moral ones that will always be primary for us. The protection of all life, especially the most vulnerable, the protection of the biblical (Genesis 2:18-24) definition of marriage as between one man and one woman and the nurture of the family, the advocacy of religious liberty, and the advocacy of sex only within marriage are crucial issues for the Christian in addressing his or her culture.

There is another constituency, though, that is looking for leadership on other important issues in order to be a blessing to all the families of the earth (Genesis 12:3). These are usually younger Christians, or more liberal ones who have learned that in order to effectively deepen our impact on society we must broaden our team.

What are these other areas addressed in the Bible that are also important to God?

- **Peace** – Jesus said, "Blessed are the peacemakers…" (Matthew 5:9). Though conflict is sometimes necessary, it is never God's ultimate choice. Ambrose and Augustine outlined a "just war" theory; its purpose was not to justify aggression but to limit it. The primary question for a Christian is never, "Do we have the right to go to war?" The primary question for a Christian is, "How can I work toward peace?"

  When the Bible talks about peace, it is not just talking about the absence of conflict, but also the building up of all of life. Peace is a term for betterment and fulfillment. So the basic value that we must voice and vote is this: How can I take the present situation (or issue or candidate) and support what will bring not only the solution to conflict but the reconciliation of people?

- **Basic Human Rights, Including Religious Liberty** – Every person is created in the image of God (Genesis 1:26-27). Each person, therefore, deserves life, liberty, and to be treated with respect. Any form of oppression that subtracts from the dignity and freedom of people is wrong. These forms include:
  - Any restriction of religious freedom
  - Any permanent class or caste system
  - Human sex trafficking and slavery
  - Failure to search for the cures of any disease that

would disable large segments of the population

    ◦   Any long-term restriction of a free market system

- **Poverty** – The Scripture doesn't just talk about giving to the poor, it talks about empowering the poor so that they can be poor no more! The famous verses found in Deuteronomy 15:11-18 (from which Jesus quotes) are really about equipping the poor so that they can be free from the benefactors some day. So the question on legislation is not merely, "What temporary relief can we give people?" (although that is often needed) but "What does this bill or candidate promise to do that will end the cycle of poverty?"

- **Creation Care (environment)** – As I have mentioned, in Genesis 2:15 God gives a simple command to mankind about the earth: "Cultivate it and keep it." That is to say we must not only be concerned with production, but also with the protection of God's creation. Dominion is never given for the purpose of exploitation. Christians, of all people, should be thankful enough for the grace of God and His immeasurable gifts that we would not want to pollute such gifts. The question for us is, "How does this candidate or bill seek to balance production with protection, or how can I be a part of preserving the earth for the generations to come?"

- **Justice Issues** – In Isaiah 61:8, as well as many other places in the Bible, God declares, "I, the Lord, love justice." Of course this has everything to do with each person being made in the image of God. It also has to do with God being a holy God Who demands that right prevail.

Ron Sider does a fine job in writing about an approach to justice. Particularly interesting to me is his definition of "Distributive Justice," which he defines as "how the numerous goods of society are divided."[1] Of course there are other types of justice, such as retributive and procedural. But the latter are more the concerns of the courts and the former more a concern of legislation.

The question from a biblical standpoint for a Christian to consider is, How much does the community or state or nation have an obligation to equip the individual for the good of all? Or, more personally, Will this legislation or candidate result in the kind of redistribution of wealth that strengthens all of society?

Improving Our Aim

We must focus on spiritual growth rather than winning elections; the aim is not power but service.

Question: How long will these election results last? Answer: Until the next election.

Question: How long does a life changed by faith and practice last?

Answer: Forever.

We all should know that addressing social policy is part of our necessary service as Christians. What may be difficult to keep in mind is that policy does not transform life's most important and precious areas. It will change circumstances, but it will not change people.

Is it a waste of time then? By no means! What Jesus had in mind when He told us to "render to Caesar" was not immediately the conversion of Caesar. Conversion of political leaders doesn't happen because citizens are contributing their voice and vote.

Jesus had in mind at least these three things: First, that the movement of Christ-followers would not be seen as political dissidents whose goal was to get out of civic responsibility (1 Peter 2:13-15). Second, that caring about government would result in the kind of environment where the Gospel could be more easily spread (1 Timothy 2:1-4). Third, that our public demonstration of our faith and service would strengthen and confirm that faith in us (James 2:17-18).

We experience a distinct kind of spiritual growth when we are serving to better the world rather than just to know God more intimately. There's a noticeable spiritual difference in a Christian who won't venture outside a small group study and a Christian who is working to improve his community (serving in a homeless shelter, participating in a campaign involving moral issues, etc.).

Of course we want our side to win. But if God is sovereign, and He is conducting the affairs of state (Daniel 2:21), then what do we have to worry about? Our main job on earth is to spread the Gospel and to help Christians mature into servants who will make others want to know the God we worship. Politics is a great venue for such service.

Advanced Intellectual and Moral Training

In the Syntopicon (a listing of great ideas) of *Great Books of the Western World*, the word "politics" is not even listed. That is because politics is simply a venue for much more important and foundational ideas to be expressed and embodied. We need to educate people about the ideas and ideals that are deeper than the issues of the day.

The religious right is known for quick reaction to pending and dangerous issues, but most conservative Christians would be more confident (and more like Christ) if they had a deeper understanding of political ideas. Societies are not changed by single political issues; issues are set by prevailing values in the culture. How do those values originate? Whoever is putting forth the "big ideals," which come from the big ideas, are the thought leaders of the culture. And when those big ideals filter throughout enough of the population, the culture changes and the political leaders follow.

Christians need to be thought leaders. We need to identify those who best express the whole of biblical values, and then we need to transfer the tools to think deeply and clearly to the general Christian population for their use in addressing the issues of the day.

Identifying intellectual and philosophical thought leaders who will clarify and advance basic Christian values is a treasure hunt. They may not be the people who are most visible and many are not even our contemporaries. But if we can read their works from time to time, we can re-orient ourselves to the eternal rather than be tossed about by every wind of current doctrine.

Of course, nothing can replace a familiarity with the classics. From Augustine to Jonathan Edwards to C.S. Lewis, from Adam Smith to Cardinal John Henry Newman, the span and depth of thought relating to culture literally cuts new pathways in our brains.

More contemporary conservative/cultural thought leaders such as Catholic intellectuals Michael Novak, Richard John Neuhaus (*First Things* journal) and Peter Kreeft, and Protestant intellectuals including Os Guinness and James Davison Hunter are starting points to examine the more permanent ideas behind the ever-changing political contests.

The big idea is one that we have heard before, but not many are paying attention yet: Christians don't need to be taught *what* to think; Christians need to be taught *how* to think biblically. Christians need to be able to transfer our ancient biblical and moral values to any field in which we choose to participate, including politics. We need to grasp the eternal concerns embedded in today's issues and political decisions. We need to recognize the recurring contest between immediate gratification and long-term consequences. And we need to be so thorough and confident in our analyses that we can promote thinking that will result in greater impact and less volume. And we need to realize that God has already put into place teachers, of millions of Christians, who can enable this process.

Mobilizing Churches, Empowering Pastors

I am a pastor. That is what I have wanted to be since shortly after my conversion. The responses to that announcement were negative. Those who knew my background of pagan behavior thought it was "a religious phase" that would pass. Those who were college think-tankers with me wondered aloud, "Why would you want to waste your intellect and abilities on such a culturally irrelevant and impotent institution as the church?"

I am a pastor. I love the church, even with all of our blemishes. Do we have more than our share of wackos? Yes, we are the only institution mandated by our Lord to accept them. (So when no one else can tolerate you, come to church.) Do we have hypocrites, shysters, self-gratifying showmen? Yes, some of them are on national TV. Why do we stand for it? Because the church is mainly a collection of people who recognize we all need a lot of work.

I am just a pastor, but I know a secret: God is going to use the church to change the world. God enjoys using the weak for the very strongest of purposes (1 Corinthians 2:1-5). And pastors, or spiritual leaders of Christian groups, must lead the way.

Pastors are both the greatest disappointment and the greatest potential in addressing society's ills. The modern church, not unlike the Titanic, has thought itself to be unsinkable and has spent much time focused on inward activities. How isolating and inconsequential even if we don't sink!

Pastors are beginning to get involved in the "welfare of the city" to which they have been sent (Jeremiah 29:4-7). The church all across the land is waking up to the fact that we are to be a blessing to all fellow citizens, and pastors are beginning to see the excitement about doing community projects that reveal the love of Christ. That kind of direct congregational mission is a terrific venue of blessing for "outsiders" and spiritual growth for "insiders." But the common understanding of mission in the church has not yet included impacting social policy.

To be honest, pastors are scared to death of politics. Now I can hear a lot of saber rattling (Bible flipping?) out there. "I'm not scared! I'm wise and protective of my flock when it comes to divisive issues!" Uh, OK. But really, pastors *are* scared. We are scared of part of our congregation criticizing us, because politics is a volatile arena and we *will* be criticized by some for even going into such teaching. We are scared of division; we are scared of misunderstanding; we are scared of being wrong. And, minor concern, we are scared of losing our jobs. Hey, what can a pastor do in the real world? (Hint: "Do you want fries with that?")

But we pastors went into our callings precisely because we wanted to make a positive difference in the world as well as in eternity. You don't become a pastor to get rich or to be praised or because you wanted to be popular and hide from controversy. (If you did enter the ministry for these reasons, then you got some really bad career counseling.) We became pastors because we love God and we love the people He loves. We became pastors because we want our lives, and the lives of those we lead, to really count for something in eternity. And we want to leave this world a better place.

So why is it, then, that the current leadership of the religious right has "church liaisons," but is not positioned to expect pastors to take the leadership for their own congregations? Most Christians in the United States, and those in the rest of the world, as well, will never become involved in the public square unless they get periodic permission, training, and encouragement from the pulpit.

I believe we can effectively motivate and mobilize pastors and spiritual leaders if we empower them with three types of capabilities that they can pass on to their congregations:

1. Pastors can be given a basic understanding of how every Christian's involvement in the public square is a biblical expectation and a key to spiritual growth. Pastors care about building people who obey God.

2. Pastors can be given materials to teach people in their congregations theologically and philosophically how to discern eternal matters and apply them to contemporary issues. These materials should be relevant to teaching from the pulpit, or in a Sunday School class or in a small group. Obviously, the pastor should not be the only teacher, but the lead teacher. Part of the teaching material should reference helpful Web-based information (see chapter 10).

3. Pastors can be given a way to organize a reference (or case studies) group where they can go for counsel or "best practices" personal advice. Many of us need grassroots colleagues when it comes to figuring out how to approach a topic in a positive, constructive, and actionable manner.

Moving Toward the Ideal

When Jesus taught, He did not create action from "the next right thing." He taught the ideal while recognizing we were working with a broken system. For example, when speaking on divorce, He first laid out the ideal, "Man ... wife ... shall become one" (Matthew 19:3-6). He then told why the law admitted exceptions for divorce (4-9).

We need not settle for less than the ideal just because we have failed so far. God has made us to be witnesses of His grace embodied in His Son (Acts 1:8) and through His church (1 Corinthians 12:27). And our witness is to extend into all areas of life, including the public square (Acts 26:26).

The church is still here to love people directly, and through godly public policy.

Notes
1. Ronald J. Sider and Diane Knippers, *Toward an Evangelical Public Policy*, (Baker Books: Grand Rapids, 2005) 165.

SIX

THE PILATE PROCESS, PART 1:

Learning to Discuss ... Without Becoming Disgusting

It is not the role of government to judge between rival systems of metaphysics and to legislate one among others. Rather, government's role is to protect and preserve a free course for its constitutional guarantees.   —Carl F.H. Henry

have wondered if being a Christian in politics and being Christlike in politics is the same. I think not. *Christian* is the name of a representative group. We are a group with vested interests in the world, interests that make it difficult for us to be objective. Christ was interested in the world—which is not the same as having interests, which need to be protected in the world. Christ could look at the world and be interested primarily in the spiritual welfare of all individuals. Christians look at the world and see "us" and "them."

There are probably many Christian approaches to politics. I would assume from the political involvement of most Christians I have seen that their strategy is identical to non-Christian groups. We Christians tend to focus on an issue or candidate, evaluate that person with our value system, accumulate a power base in reaction, and do what we can for or against. That is how politics works, and that seems to be how Christian politics works. Perhaps there is a difference afterward in the way the country runs; perhaps not. But is there a difference afterward in the way people view Christ? Perhaps Christians have more respect and power after a political battle; perhaps not. But is their reflection of God one that becomes Him, and is their witness one that pleases Him?

There would be great advantage in finding a Christlike approach to politics. The advantage would not necessarily be for the Christians, but, when all was said and done, it would glorify God. Just as the scriptural principle of righteousness makes it clear that we must be involved, we also need a scriptural process, a way to be involved. But "scriptural process" here means learning from and applying Scripture and not just quoting verses. Certainly any Christian approach should be within the guidelines of Scripture. But a Christlike approach will not emphasize guidelines nearly as much as relationships. Establishing "Christian values" was not the ultimate goal of Christ; people have always been His goal. Christian values are the framework that strengthens relationships. It is much easier to be right than it is to love, but a Christlike approach to politics emphasizes benefits to people over benefits of power.

A Christian approach to politics may show those in opposition just how wrong their opposition is. The Christlike approach to politics respectfully acknowledges the points at which they are right. A Christian approach could tell everyone how to vote; the Christlike approach directs the attention of the voters to underlying values. A Christian approach could give us certainty; the Christlike approach gives us a biblical perspective.

It seems reasonable, when investigating how to face politics in a Christlike manner, to turn to the record of the main event in which Christ faced politics. In returning to that event we can extract a picture of Christ's approach, Pilate's mistakes, and God's success. With that picture in mind we can discern a practical approach to address every political situation. I call this "The Pilate Process" to remind us how we often miss the point of political confrontations. Its basic objective is to give individuals a means to approach issues or candidates in ways that will not miss the point. The Pilate Process will help us determine what we believe, why we believe it, and why we believe it is of God. The practical result will be that many individuals will be able to become both competent and Christlike in a political setting. The government will not only sense a large Christian grassroots concern; the general population will see a selfless political approach. What a witness that will be!

Why Identify with Pilate?

Some of us will have difficulty identifying with Pilate. After all, he was not very much like us, was he? Well, maybe a few of his more obvious traits will sound familiar. As we read Matthew 27:11-26, Mark 15:1-15, Luke 23:1-25, and John 18:28-19:22, we may identify with some of his tendencies. First, even though Pilate was in the position of being politically responsible, he was not at all excited about addressing religiopolitical issues. He was not looking for trouble; his life seemed best when the status quo was maintained. He had plenty to do and was not searching for additional agenda. When confronted with this religiopolitical issue, this candidate for king of the Jews, he knew it was his job to decide the case. But he decided to avoid deciding. He put it back upon the religious people who had raised the issue in the first place. They were the ones with the heartburn, he assumed, so let them take care of the matter: "Take Him yourselves, and judge Him" (John 18:31). But they tossed the matter back to him, claiming that they alone could not do what needed to be done. Pilate then tried to pass the matter on to Herod (Luke 23:7-12). Herod stamped "Return to Sender" on the case. If the religiously agitated couldn't handle the matter, and if the rest of the political system avoided the matter, maybe it was Pilate's responsibility to decide. So he did decide, but he did not take responsibility. He let custom tender his decision (Matthew 27:15). He let the crowd reverse his judgment (Luke 23:16, 25). He let excuse replace action (Matthew 27:24).

Perhaps Pilate is not so different from us in his avoidance of the religiopolitical issues. We who are citizen-rulers avoid those issues because they are so much trouble. We tend to leave it to our beloved political system or to a majority who neither recognizes nor cares about Christ. We may say, "I'll leave it to the religious activists, since they are so interested," only to have them say, "We need your help." Our reasons for avoidance may be similar to Pilate's.

Pilate had a tendency to fear what might happen to his relationships if he were involved in religious politics. He had family pressure not to get involved (Matthew 27:19). There could be job repercussions if he were connected with such controversial matters (John 19:12). Pilate was also getting all stirred up inside; his peace with himself was challenged (John 19:7-8). It is no wonder that Pilate dreaded religiopolitical issues, or that we do. Some of those issues may demand a price far greater than we are willing to pay. When we are from time to time confronted with

such situations we will make our choice. We can learn much
from Pilate's mistakes and even more from Christ's example. Let
us now turn to the six-step Christian political approach called
The Pilate Process.

STEP 1: Get away from confrontational demonstration — to think.

I define a *demonstration* as one or more people confronting us
with a political issue. The confrontation has the effect of arousing
our emotions and capturing our attention. For Pilate, both Jesus,
the controversial religious leader, and the mob who brought Him
were demonstrations.

The primary step in addressing religiopolitical situations is to
calm down so the atmosphere will permit reason. Like booster
rockets, demonstrations tend to perform one valuable act. They
boost a singular issue above the other issues into a place where all
can see and pay attention. Like booster rockets, demonstrations
have one major liability: after they have done their work, they
are dead weight. After the booster has done its job it should
detach from the craft. If that doesn't happen there is going to be
trouble.

Pilate's major mistakes began with his assumption that he could
reason in that setting with those demonstrators. He discovered
how perpetually inflammatory a situation can become when a
major religious figure or issue is put in a political setting. Yet
intentional demonstrations are more for show than for reason.
Demonstrators desire to have a point understood, not debated.
Speaking as a veteran of demonstrations during the 1960s, I
cannot remember a single demonstration whose crowd was
open to or desired reason. Demonstrations are valuable only for

making a point. Demonstrations are given to excess when asked to do more than they are capable of doing. In considering the crowd, let us understand political demonstrations to the extent that we can both use them and avoid being used by them.

Are political demonstrations bad? If demonstrations were deemed inherently evil, we would need to ban both the Republican and Democratic conventions. They are, basically, political demonstrations orchestrated to get points across to the American people. Establishment demonstrations are no less ludicrous than antiestablishment demonstrations are. We can tune in to the next major political party conventions and watch what happens after the words, "I give you the next president of the United States, _____!" Bands play, balloons fall down (or rise up), people dressed in costumes dance, shrill horns shriek, and people parade, carrying signs that show their allegiance. What is the point of all this? They are there to motivate themselves and to convince others they are right. If we were to switch channels to the news program, we might see a strikers' picket line outside a factory or a citizens' picket line outside a courthouse. Each is making its point publicly, with signs and some costumes as well. When the Constitution of the United States gave us the right of assembly (First Amendment), it was guarding our right to demonstrate.

The good of demonstrations becomes evident when we realize that most people, like Pilate, will not take action on any issue until confronted. Common sense and experience tell us that our involvement increases proportionately to the sense of importance we attach to any issue. Numerous political surveys confirm this link: "Persons are more likely to turn out for elections they perceive to be important."[1] Demonstrations are a way to move a particular issue up the value scale of the intended audience, and a way of provoking response. Would the Vietnam War have ended as quickly without all of the demonstrations that caused political pressure? Probably not. No matter what side of that issue we were on, most would readily admit that the demonstrations were what moved the American people, and eventually the government, to end the war. Would we have the advancements in civil rights today without the demonstrations of the 1960s? Probably not. From the sympathy evoked by pictures of police dogs tearing into peaceful marchers, to the fear evoked by the race riots, our attention was captured. The government was also confronted by those demonstrations, and legislation plus favorable court decisions resulted.

Deliberation after Demonstration. So demonstrations have been and will continue to be valuable. Yet there is a major principle for us all to keep in mind: *Improvements may be made because of demonstrations but are seldom made in the midst of demonstrations.* Jesus withdrew from the crowds for deliberation, but Pilate stood in the midst of the crowd while making his choices. Unlike Pilate, thinking people must distance political decision and action from the emotionalism of the masses. Jesus chose not to add to the fiery atmosphere though He was in the midst of the demonstration. Emotionalism, rather than deliberation, tends to rule at demonstrations. An incident in which hundreds of Christians desired to legitimately demonstrate their opposition to a zoning variance illustrates the point.

I sat in a county council's meeting room for a board of adjustments meeting. Although the meetings usually had limited attendance, this night the room was overflowing into the hall. Word had come to the Christians in our area that a new establishment—the "Erotic" something or other—was trying to get a zoning variance. The establishment would not only rent pornographic movies (something that most video clubs in the area were already doing) but would also have "live entertainment." That was new to the area and unwanted by a majority of Christians. Many Christians had come to voice opposition; a few had brought their children.

As the proceedings began, the chairman issued a sensible opening statement to this effect: "I know that many of you are here to voice opposition to this establishment. The board would appreciate it if you would have representative speakers for groups. Please be brief. You will be heard, but when the speeches begin to become repetitive in content, we will end the discussion period to decide the matter." The attorney for the "Erotic" business made his case in a calm and reasoned manner—very polite, very respectable. His point was basically that his client's store would not offer anything that other video stores in the area were not offering except "maybe one or two girls." The obscenity law of the county was new and untested, he implied, and it would be a shame to have to go to court and have it smashed. He was slick. The implication was that an agreeable decision now would save a court battle and a loss of time and revenue.

When he finished, the floor was open for discussion. I was seated (providentially, I think) beside a Christian attorney who was a veteran of many political confrontations in the community at large. He knew I had lived in the area only a year and a half, so he kept me informed privately as the "discussion" progressed publicly.

"Are there any to speak for this business?" the chairman asked. A moment of silence followed as "who would dare?" glances shot around the room. "No one," came the unspoken answer.

"Who will speak against it?" the chairman asked. A gray-haired man in a brown polyester suit raised his hand. "That's one of three political preachers in the area," my attorney guide whispered. "Whenever there is a public forum, a place to be seen and heard on a controversial matter, you usually find them there." The man stood to give a surprisingly brief statement. For a moment I relaxed.

Then I found myself dreading the inevitable: a Christian who would stand and say or do something silly enough to erase the positive impact of the simple presence of 200 Christian citizens. This happened quickly enough.

A big man walked down to the front of the meeting hall. He was carrying a brown paper bag. *Oh, no*, I thought, *here it comes*.

"That's another one of our political preachers," whispered my guide.

Oh, no, I repeated to myself.

The fellow's face was flushed. He began to speak partly to the board members, partly to the crowd, but mostly to the TV camera. "Do any of you have any idea of the kind of filth we are talking about here? I stopped by a store to buy this pornographic magazine, (*Oh no! Oh no! Oh no!*) and I just want you to cast your eyes on this smut!" With that he whirled around to flash the pictures to an unready audience. I cannot fully describe the effect on the audience because I could not tell how many were closing their eyes in purity or how many were squinting for better focus. I do know that all felt like they were in a situation out of control. As the demonstrator talked on (most were too shocked to hear what he said), he turned again to show the picture directly into the TV camera. His barrage of "righteous indignation" finally ended.

He returned to his seat with his reloaded brown paper bag.

Several more spoke against the zoning variance. A chief of police spoke about the possibilities of increased crime. A counselor spoke about his work with those who had been significantly harmed by their use of pornography. A man stood to give an account of the sexual acts he had seen performed in such an establishment. The discussion grew more consuming. Then, in one final blaze of heat (but not light), a man swaggered to the front. "I am not one of these Christians," he began. "But we all know what kind of vermin go into these places!" "Amen!" came a call from his religious counterpart. "They are not even human," he continued. "Anyone that goes into one of these places is garbage. They are worms, and worse! There is nothing decent about them, and we don't want that human trash around here! They are _____nothings!"

Something strange happened at this point. It was like a slap in our collective face. Many, I learned afterward, were embarrassed to be linked with that kind of emotional excess and derogatory verbiage. Many of us returned to our cars wishing the point could have been made intelligently, calmly, and with respect for all persons involved. I am not sure that calm, intelligent behavior is possible in a political demonstration that invites all to participate. If it were possible to have demonstrations orchestrated in such a manner, at least two benefits would be ours. First, the credibility we gain from those who might oppose us would be remarkable. The tone of voice used by the chairman of that board of adjustments betrayed a combination of condescension and anticipation. He might as well have said, "I know what you are going to say and how you are going to say it before you even begin" to the Christians who had come to demonstrate their concern. What a difference for him it would have made if we had organized to the point where two or three persons could have spoken for us in terms that would address his intelligence and sense of values!

Second, orchestrated demonstrations would ensure more Christians participating. My wife, who had never been on a picket line in her life, went with me to a one-hour picket line in front of the "Erotic" whatever when it opened in spite of being denied the zoning variance. We did not want to carry a sign, we did not want to chant, we did not want to say clever things to people entering the store. We just wanted to protest what we saw as a violation of community standards and the law. But, midway in the picket time, one of the political preachers brought in a casket with a skeleton in it. The skeleton was named Philip or Phyllis Porno. And when a TV camera arrived (that is the point of a demonstration — to be seen), the cameraman went straight to the casket, and then started filming all of us. Most Christians want to avoid those kinds of tacky tactics, believing them to be counterproductive. Many who would stand up for their faith intelligently explained will not stand for their faith being so shabbily summarized.

Nevertheless, demonstrations have and will continue to serve a positive purpose. They bring to the attention of all, Christians included, issues that would otherwise be ignored. They prompt people to action. To be ultimately effective, though, we must detach ourselves from them. Unlike Pilate, we must let their value lie solely in the fact that they have captured our attention. Reason based upon the passion of a demonstration usually turns out to be not reason at all, but reaction.

If the demonstration is a group of people instead of a

candidate, we can prepare the demonstration stage for purposes of higher thought in several ways. The most effective way is separating the time of the demonstration from the time we make the decision about the issue. Pilate felt hard-pressed for an immediate decision. He may have feared that riot or bad reports to Caesar would result if he did not make a decision immediately. He was provoked to react instead of reason. Pilate feared for his safety, his reputation, and his job. Emotional provocation centers the basis for decision making on us, not on the issue at hand. While that is understandable and valid, it is only part of the consideration. Time is needed to quell the inner fears. We need to ask rational questions like, What is best for the common good? or, What is the opposite side to the one being presented by the demonstration? or, What do the emotions in me have to do with the issues at hand?

Separation of confrontation and thinking implies not only time but space. A Christian can avoid Pilate's mistake by postponing a decision and separating physically from the demonstration. Scripture has recorded that every time Pilate had contact with Jesus, he was at the same time, or almost the same time, relating to the Jewish demonstrators. At one point, the demonstrators were not present, so he called them together (Luke 23:13). Such a proximity to the voices calling for a certain action hardly allows for calm reflection on the matter. We have the same tendency as Pilate when we do not consider or research political issues in private but make up our minds while talking to or watching people who are trying to convince us. Whether they are face-to-face with us, or they are entering our living rooms through the television, we must not be intimidated into a position that is a reaction. We can walk away to think; we can turn off the television to talk with a variety of others. That way much of the pressure of the demonstration can fade.

And while we are taking some time in separation from whatever forced our attention to the issue, we can dilute that force by considering alternate opinions. Demonstrations appear to be shouting, "There are only two alternatives in this matter, ours and the one against us. Now decide which side you are on!" There is scriptural evidence that Pilate tried to get creative enough to get around agreeing or disagreeing with the demonstrators. He did come up with the Barabbas alternative so that the demonstrators themselves would relieve him of the decision. His mistake, however, was that he never changed the basic "for or against" mentality. He never stopped to consider the deeper question of truth or sought out other opinions on the issue of Jesus. He never tested the singular, powerful voice of the demonstration against other voices and opinions which would have created some balance in deliberation. Indeed, it seldom occurs to any of us that we do not have to take a given side in order to take a stand. We are in a position to collect various insights. We are not confined to an ultimatum. Far from adding confusion, taking time to note others' opinions will put our political decisions in a new category. We may be able to add insight instead of only receiving it. And the stand we finally take will be truly ours instead of "theirs." Broadening our basis for decision dilutes not only the pressure to decide; it makes more potent the capacity to decide with accuracy.

STEP 2: Overlook a narrow religious perspective.

Truth is stranger than fiction; truth is also stronger than friction. It seems logical to assume that Christianity is strongest when it is most forceful. It is also seems logical to assume that if the Christian tradition is under attack, we should fight back. It is almost inconceivable that, at a point where religion is most desperately needed, we would detach ourselves from religious terms. It would be so natural to respond to mockery with a counterattack.

Both Jesus and the religious crowd were threatened but the two reacted differently. The Jews tried to protect their religion by complaining to the authorities. They organized as much political force as they could muster. They mobilized a campaign to save the country, a campaign based on accusation, negativism, and fear. They won the debate, and missed the point.

Jesus, on the other hand, offered no defense. He was not interested in justifying Himself. He was interested in truth. "For this I have been born, and for this I have come into the world, to bear witness to the truth. Everyone who is of the truth hears my voice" (John 18:37). He used no religious talk. He used the highest universal goal, the truth, and was confident that those seeking the truth would understand Him. Such a strategy made Him vulnerable; such a strategy made Him invincible.

It is sobering today to find Christians choosing the former political strategy of the crowd instead of the latter demonstrated by Jesus. It will cost us more than we realize. If we choose to defend our religion rather than seek the whole truth, we will lose three very important capacities: We will lose our ability to see God outside of our own tradition; We will lose our capacity to influence people, in any positive sense, toward God; We will lose the opportunity to grow in our own faith.

A young lady once came into my office to ask me questions about our local church. She was trying to decide whether or not to attend. One of the first questions she asked was, "How big a God do you believe in?" I knew what she meant. If we are not more interested in truth than in our traditional expressions of religion, we can miss seeing who God really is. Our tendency is to see our church traditions as something we need to protect rather than something we need to look through. It is like keeping the protective caps on binoculars while we are using them. We can either protect the lenses that were made to enhance our vision, or we can use them to bring closer what is distant. We cannot do both at once. We cannot see the issues for what they are, or the candidates for who they are, if we limit our look to our past. God may be doing "a new thing." The question we must ask is, "How could God be involved in this issue or candidate to accomplish His purpose?" Answering that question takes searching.

The mandate for this searching comes from Jesus. In His trial process He tells the chief priests to look beyond that single glimpse of Him and to search for the whole truth about Him: "Why do you question Me? Question those who have heard what I spoke to them" (John 18:21). The statement is an extension of the research process He mentioned previously, recorded in John 5:31-37. The process acknowledges the limitations of a person being his own witness (5:31). The process entails looking to predecessors (5:33) and recent colleagues (18:21). It also advises that we look at one's deeds (5:36) and rely upon the witness of the Spirit. The process is not only a valid guideline for objectively appraising candidates today; it reminds us that as we search for the whole truth about someone, we will be able to see more clearly how God would have us vote. We cannot just listen to a candidate's statements on religious issues and claim to know the candidate adequately. There are professional and personal aspects of a candidate's life that should be taken into account when we enter the voting booth. You will find several of those in chapter nine. Research on the candidates is important because offices do not make laws, people do. We are not depending on offices to govern us with sound judgment, wisdom, and integrity. We are trusting the people we elect to those offices. So we need to know if those people have integrity. It is not unusual for a candidate disgraced by his own actions to tell the American people that he wishes everyone would just concentrate on the issues instead of on him. But in the truest sense, the person *is* the issue. The person who is a candidate *is* the issue that will determine for us all the other issues. While it is true that a morally good person can make a poor official, we can't expect that the opposite might be true. Is it reasonable to assume that a person with an immoral private life will make moral decisions while in office? Possible, but unlikely.

On the other hand, narrow-minded religious concerns cannot grasp the whole picture. The broader our perspective, the more we can see of God's potential purpose. Interest in only one area can cause us to ignore much valid information. Studies done over a period of sixteen years found that "the partisan is not really interested in messages from both sides: primarily partisans pick up messages from their own side."[2] But Christ calls us to learn the whole truth before we can see what God is doing.

The strategy of defending a religious tradition also eliminates our capacity to positively influence other people toward God. When we are so narrowly focused upon our own concerns, we cannot expect others to really hear us. The religious crowd that presented their concerns to Pilate was clearly purposed in defending their religion and political advantage. The charges they presented were significant crimes. Not only did they charge that He was misleading the nation, but that He was also "forbidding to pay taxes to Caesar, and saying that He Himself is . . . a King" (Luke 23:2). Pilate did not investigate; he hardly heard. Instead, he promptly declared, "I find no guilt in this man" (Luke 23:4). How could he decide so fast? Pilate reacted not to their statements but to their motivation. Pilate could see that their motivation was envy (Matthew 27:18). He had no trouble perceiving that their political ends were focused upon their own benefit. He had no desire to help them or join them in their goals.

Christians defending a religious tradition are similarly dismissed. And why shouldn't we be? The world does not give a hoot about our religion, and they will not give one until they perceive that we care more about all people than our own interests. If evangelicals in politics cause people to dismiss Christianity because of our defense of it, how tragic that is!

We are called to be witnesses (Acts 1:8), to point beyond ourselves. Christ shows us two important prerequisites to witnessing. First, we need to get rid of the counterattack mentality. Counterattack not only kills our own search for truth, it kills everyone else's as well. Jesus quietly and calmly told the truth when under fire. The truth was His strength. He did not need any other justification. "But Jesus made no further answer; so that Pilate was amazed" (Mark 15:5). In contrast, counterattack simply solidifies separate positions, and no positive influence can flow from it. Though there was no evident influence in His trial process, Jesus never switched strategies. His attitude never hardened, and it kept no one who was interested away.

The second prerequisite Jesus modeled was His use of nonreligious language. Religious terms can shut people out. Why then do we insist on speaking "Christianese?" We may hope that quoting Scripture, chapter and verse, to back up our points, or shouting "Amen!" to a speech will communicate something of the Spirit to people. It does communicate a spirit—a spirit of exclusion, because the words we've chosen have the meaning we intend, only to others of our own group. Because Jesus realized the vast difference between the spiritual world and the earthly world (John 18:36) He used a term that is universally understood and attractive: truth.

The search for truth in any issue or candidate puts religious and nonreligious on common ground. As any Christian who is honest with himself knows, the revealed truth of Scripture does not automatically transfer onto the contemporary issues of our nation. It does not replace the gathering of facts. It does not save us from the need to calculate the consequences of our vote. Scripture does not relieve us from the need to draw truth from those with a different perspective. All truth is God's truth. The search for truth is hampered by any special lingo that would make communication unwelcome or more difficult. Any statement we make that sounds religious rather than moral creates walls.

A real test of Christianity in politics is this: Are a great variety of people benefited by our political stance, even people who are not of our faith? We are following the footsteps of Christ when we work hard to assist others, even when their political stance is different from our own, and when we talk in terms that communicate to everyone.

It is important that we not be blocked from growing in our faith. Both language and our desire for wisdom are important aspects of our spiritual growth. Language does not just describe reality, it molds our perception of reality. So phrasing descriptions of political problems in only religious language limits our ability to conceptualize those problems. Religious language so necessary in describing the "other realm" (spiritual concerns) may not exactly fit "this realm." Therefore we could miss much, not just in relation to other people but in relation to our own understanding, if compelled to stick with religious terms for political analysis.

Opposing views often help clarify our points and force us to reframe them in broader language, which is great for our intellectual growth and spiritual witness.

We will get stronger as the battle wears on, not more drained. He will expand our spirit, our influence, and our intellect. We will be able to examine God's whole truth, and He will add immeasurably to the faith in Him that we have now.

STEP 3: Observe deep principles rather than shallow politics.

The religious crowd missed the truth because they were too focused on religion. Pilate missed it because he was too focused on politics. Looking at issues and candidates only as religious conduits is wrong. Thinking through candidates' strategies and issues will always help us in searching for truth.

Politics is the art of fixing conflict. It can be more than that, but it seldom is. Pilate typified the temptation to temporarily quell a disturbance rather than make a decision that would stand the test of time. Pilate thought of a quick solution, not a principle. He thought in terms of relief, not cure.

The great benefit Christians should be able to bring to the American political process is one of depth. Those who see the world in more than one dimension, who think in ages longer than this life, are valuable voices. The basis of our decision to follow Christ was that we would live in light of the future. That basis is also best for politics but quite rare in politics. Politics, as Pilate knew, gets so complicated that the attention shifts to the details of the moment rather than the results long term. Politics is compromise. Politics is swapping favors. At times the process involves the very real ultimatum, "You can secure your own political future, or you can do what you know to be right." The threat in John 19:12 reflects this practical-versus-principle battle. The crowd threatens Pilate by saying, "If you release this man, you are no friend of Caesar." He was hearing that his political life was at stake. We need not be too critical when we read the next verse: "When Pilate heard these words, he brought Jesus out." Political officeholders, unlike many of their constituents, put their reputations (and hence their jobs) on the line with their votes. It is far from being in an easy position. The alternatives sometimes seem to be that they either do what will keep them in office or they play the role of martyr, dying a political death for a good cause.

We are being killed by our weakness for stopgap measures and temporary fixes. We are engaged in convenience thinking rather than consequential thinking. We also do not seem to realize that every action we take is a precedent.

The convenience-versus-consequences thinking sounds like a neat cliche from a flippant sermon. It is actually a form of immaturity that has dire side effects. In the beginning of our country's history, our leaders were aware that we were an "experiment." We were not sure whether or not we had much of a future, so in the decision making we took much care to consider the consequences. The population at large did not demand convenience, or reflexively link government with their personal problems. Life was a struggle, and everyone knew it. The survival of the country was part of the population's concern. We have, of course, "progressed." Since the industrial revolution enabled us to think of jelly as well as bread, and since the victories in World War II gave us not just confidence of survival but the arrogance of a superpower, the country's survival seldom enters our minds. As personal and national survival ceased to be an issue, convenience took its place. With the help of modern technology, convenience has almost obliterated the notion of consequence. We can have sex without pregnancy and sweetness without sugar. We now have the option of developing the attitude of "all things being equal, I'd rather have whatever makes my life easier and more fun." The only time this attitude may be suspended is when group survival is again the issue.

When Pilate saw his decision in terms of his own convenience, in terms of his own political life, he did not consider that if the claims of Christ were true, the consequences of his action meant his spiritual condemnation. Was Jesus really on trial that day? Hardly. Pilate was. Every decision that relieves us of an individual responsibility has a price. Others, including our children, will have to pay it. In a very real sense, we too are on trial.

Identifying issues in terms deeper than politics also means coming to grips with this fact: each action we take sets a precedent. Our entire judicial system judges primarily on the basis of legal precedents. The strategies of successful candidates on the legislative issues seem to us to be very changeable. We tend to think, *We'll see if this works. If it doesn't, we'll change.* But the trend a candidate sets, or the mark a piece of legislation makes on our direction, is indelible. Once we take action, even though we realize later that action may have been unwise, it is easier for us to take it again. How many times did Pilate go back to the crowd to make a decision, even though he knew they had not come to the right decision previously? Three times he knowingly made the same mistake. Every act taken, indeed every option considered, becomes a precedent for its twin in the near future.

Those who follow Christ can bring much-needed reminders that principles should guide practicality, not the other way around. On the major issues we need to ask our representatives what principles are guiding specific decisions. Officeholders are special people and need special attention. As in any job, the daily routine can confine their concern to what works, and principles can be forgotten. Reminders are in order, and Christians who live their lives based on deeper-than-surface concerns are the part of "We, the people" who will ask those important questions.

Too much religious activity toward government is antagonistic. Christian interest groups are too often like all others. But the Christlike may want to do as Jesus did and bring up the deeper-than-action side of the issue to our officials. We may want to write them and ask, What are the long-lasting principles by which you have taken action on _____? Are there any moral or religious principles involved as you see it? What do you hope it will resolve years from now? Can you point to the truth of the matter for me? We might cause some reflection that will do us all good.

Notes

1. Lester W. Milbrath and M.I. Goel, *Political Participation: How and Why Do People Get Involved in Politics?* (Chicago: Rand McNally, 1977), 40.

SEVEN
THE PILATE PROCESS, PART 2:
Moving From Awareness to Personal Participation

Be to the world a sign that, while we as Christians do not have all the answers, we do know and care about the questions.

—Billy Graham

Let's be honest ... for most of us politics is confusing, boring, or futile. Oh, it is not terribly difficult to fulfill the first of the demands of our citizenship: awareness. Television news, Internet news sites, daily newspapers, and news magazines can each be the demonstration that confronts us with issues. If we are very fortunate, our local church may even provide information about religiopolitical issues. And the first three steps of The Pilate Process do not require Herculean effort. We would willingly detach from the demonstration and examine the issues with more breadth than one religious tradition and more depth than what is politically expedient. That is, we would examine them if we had the time, or if we were in the right mood, or if we were forced by emergency.

Awareness of the issues gives us the ability to respond, but we need more. The difference between *response ability* and *responsibility* is roughly that of putting an "i" in the gap. Most people drop out at this point. Pilate did.

Pilate, like many people, used the political process to hide. He rationalized that his anonymity might help achieve unanimity, which was better for the country. That should have worked out very nicely for Pilate, as it should for us. If the issue turned out well, he could reap the benefits. If the issue turned out badly, he could not be blamed. So Pilate claimed, "I am innocent . . . see to that yourselves" (Matthew 27:24). Then he disappeared into neutrality.

Like Pilate, many of us have legitimate, even powerful, reasons for not taking action on what we know. Our reluctance may stem from our lack of definite solutions. And the issues *are* complicated. Pilate's job was not only to think about justice, but also to maintain peace. In the case of Jesus, these political goals were conflicting. We, too, face those complicated, no-easy-answer issues. We desire to help the helpless of our nation without accommodating freeloaders. We desire a strong national defense, but we want to avoid a militant mentality that will send our children into unnecessary combat (or nuclear holocaust). We desire to have the government provide necessary services, but the national debt not only threatens economic collapse but also reflects our national tendency not to delay gratification. Few of us feel qualified to define "necessary services" for all, and none of us feel a definition is coming fast enough from our political leaders. How does one respond to such a complex situation? Most would say, "I don't know. You decide," and drop out of the conversation.

If we cannot solve the political problems, which have secondary moral implications, perhaps we would fare better in the religiopolitical issues, which have primarily moral implications. We desire to save the unborn, protect traditional marriage, care for creation, and preserve the values foundational to our life together as a nation—all while not imposing our religion on others. We are against the exploitation of people by pornography, while also being against trends of government censorship. Simply put, every major issue is complicated. It is no wonder we leave the answers to the crowd. The answers may be up to us, but they are beyond us—so we quit. Then we find out what Pilate found out—others have even worse solutions.

The transition from awareness to personal, responsible participation is difficult. Most of us are not inclined in that direction and we will do whatever is convenient to avoid it. We are not a society where the traditional means of political motivation works anymore. We are not moved by duty, or guilt, or the gradual deterioration of society. The American Christian can be motivated to act politically in brief intervals by crisis or scandal. But after a brief period of personal, responsible participation, we sink back into the crowd.

One transition from awareness to participation will work: prayer.

STEP 4: Decide from prayer and scriptural principles.

Most of us begin with three major obstacles when considering political involvement. First, we wonder what it will profit us in relation to what it will cost us. Second, we wonder how much or how little responsibility is really "mine." Third, we wonder what the correct answers are to the really complex issues. Only prayer and deliberation steeped in Scripture can resolve all three obstacles:

God Transforms the "I." The *I*, the Ego described earlier, is hungry for power, domination, and self-protection. That *I*

SEVEN – THE PILATE PROCESS, PART 2

will pervert any instrument for justice into one for personal advantage. That *I* was Pilate, and that *I* can be the American Christian who will not carry out any political decision or area of work in a way that will benefit others over self. "Well," some will say, "that is the American system. The Founding Fathers planned for such selfish goals. That is why we have a system of checks and balances. People will be people; the horribly selfish *I* will always be seen at the center of political efforts." That sounds like profound realism; it is rot.

Christians, take warning. Although the American system is realistic in supposing that power groups will be the norm in our country, we are not called to be one of them. Being a special interest group is not necessarily synonymous with being a self-centered interest group. Special could really mean special in terms of character as well as concern. The evil *I* can be transformed. The cost of transformation is submission to Christ.

The malignant *I* that seeks supremacy can be transformed into the selfless servant that expects the personal cost to exceed the political benefit. Such transformation is God's hallmark for those who listen.

God Assigns the Specifics. Like Pilate, Christians tend toward an "all or nothing" approach to politics. Many do not want to get involved because they believe they could easily become overwhelmed with all of the problems. Yet prayer will also result in defined assignments and boundaries.

"The people" do have a huge responsibility. Think of the general stewardship command of Genesis 1:28, instructing people to "rule over . . . the earth." The scope of responsibility was much larger than any individual's ability. That is why God eventually instituted government and why we only have a part.

To discover what part, and how large a part, we must progress to Genesis 2:15. In that passage God gives a specific call to a specific person for a specific area of responsibility: "Then the Lord God took the man and put him into the garden of Eden to cultivate it and keep it." Our political involvement is part of how we accomplish that.

The different parts of our work—family, church, business, politics —will vary from person to person and even from season to season.

God Directs the Decisions. We want answers. And we want to make sure our answers are correct. Like Pilate, we find it easier to hear the answers of the crowd than to receive the answers from God. Yet prayer that has been informed by the news and based on the Bible is the Christian's way toward the correct personal decision. Any other method tends to produce the crowd's decision in disguise. God desires that individuals follow Him and no other (Exodus 20:3). That is not easy, but voting booths and prayer closets have much in common.

Voting booths are made for one person. Many of us can remember the first time we stepped inside a voting booth. Voting seemed like such an awesome responsibility to me that I felt less than adequate to make up my mind. Maybe, if I could have taken a group of people into the booth, we together could have made a wiser choice than I alone. There were so many names I did not recognize. There were issues numbered and levered, issues to which I had given little thought. I felt the need for a group of people to give me information about my choices. Later in life I would learn where best to access that information. But the rules were clear—one person to a booth.

There is a public-private conflict inherent in the structure of American politics. The political ideal calls individuals to make decisions for the good of the whole group. Political strategy tries to persuade individuals to make those decisions on the basis of loyalty to a particular subgroup's interests. The first requires the person to act as an individual; the second influences him not to think as an individual.

Group thinking is as attractive to many individuals as it is to political strategists. Group thinking can eliminate the uncomfortable process of individual study of the Scriptures, contemplation and prayer. It can also eliminate the threat of ostracism. In 1956, I remember watching television with my grandfather. A program having to do with the presidential election prompted me to announce to my grandfather that I was old enough to have a political opinion. "If I could vote," I said confidently, "I'd be for Ike." My grandfather flinched. "Oh, no, Joey," he said in a tone filled with pain for not having taught me better. "You couldn't do that!" "Why not?" I asked, expecting to hear some dastardly news about Ike. My grandfather replied, "Because he's a Republican and we are Democrats!" Class dismissed.

Group-based voting has a strong, if deteriorating, history in our country. More specifically, religious group-based voting has a stronger precedent than most of us have been taught. In the beginning days of our country, it would have been no surprise to find people voting on the basis of their religious group given the intense sectarianism of the earliest communities. But also from the mid-nineteenth century to the present, religious group-based voting has been found to be a factor. Robert Booth Fowler has recorded what historians have found:

> Religious divisions, often inseparably tied to ethnic differences, drew the political lines on the American map. The divisions were principally between pietists vs. nonpietists

(or ritualists). Pietists included Methodists, Baptists (if not Southern), and less liturgical Lutherans. They were almost overwhelmingly Republican regardless of where they lived. . . . On the other hand, Roman Catholics, liturgical Lutherans, and most Germans (Lutheran, Reformed, Catholic, but not pietist) stood on the other side and were usually Democrats. . . . Pietists were frankly moralistic in their understanding of religion. They saw themselves led to reform people and America and they rarely had much hesitation in proposing to use the State, its laws and policies, to accomplish their ends. Nonpietists, on the other hand, tended to emphasize church rituals and sacraments as more important to their conception of religion than moral crusades. They also had a notable easygoing (in comparison with pietists) attitude about human behavior and consistently proved more tolerant and less interested in government regulation of personal behavior . . . a good deal of the politics of the second half of the nineteenth century encouraged as well as reflected religious-ethnic divisions in the country. Especially as the decades went by and the pietists more and more felt threatened.[1]

While it is difficult to discern how much religious group-based voting is based on religion rather than other factors, it is not difficult to assume the importance of religion as a source of voter identity. We may also assume that individuals still desire to go along with a larger group when deciding on religious issues. So voting on the basis of one's religious group has both a history and a current attraction, especially in the holiness camp. The Holy Spirit leads us to a personal motive for voting. Biblical values that cause us to be pro-life, pro-family, pro-environment, pro-protection for the most vulnerable, etc. are a valid basis upon which to evaluate candidates and issues.

The Pilate Process would question the value of group decision making. Both Pilate and the religious crowd made their decisions about Jesus on the basis of their group identity. It was not just that they were caught up in a demonstration. They missed the truth because they were not open to accepting all the facts and they had the wrong guides. The religious crowd listened solely to their religious leaders. "The chief priests and the elders persuaded the multitudes to ask for Barabbas, and to put Jesus to death" (Matthew 27:20). All who were involved were under tremendous pressure to conform to a predetermined political decision. And Pilate, a representative of the Roman Empire, was not much more free from his own group identity. As an individual, though, he had a decision to make. He could have made it on the basis of his closeness to Jesus, but he was a member of the ruling party. History had dealt him a most important hand, but at the mere mention of Caesar he folded.

Politics is essentially a group activity. But, as with religion, it must be primarily an individual decision tied to a heart for people and unwavering values from Scripture.

When we are alone, the issue can have our focused attention. In public we are hurried to a "yea" or "nay." In private the question, What shall I do with this candidate or issue? has time to sink way down to where the Holy Spirit dwells. We can trust the Holy Spirit to guide us. He will bring to our minds what Christ has said (John 14:26) and all that Christ is now saying (John 16:14-15). He will speak in our hearts where Scripture is hidden (Psalm 119:11) and where it is available to apply. He will guide us into all the truth (John 16:13).

Whether God leads all praying Christians to vote the same is not the point. Living all of life like Jesus is the point. One truth stands self-evident: the unity we seek will certainly never come from politics or human agreement. If it is unity for which we hope, our only hope is in the Holy Spirit. God does not speak with a forked tongue. Eventually we will all hear the same thing from Him. But first we must train ourselves to think like Christ (1 Corinthians 2:16). To let Him be our guide in personal decisions about everything including politics is the difficult but ultimate commitment.

STEP 5: ACT!

If we know what the Bible says and have a direct leading in prayer and we do not take action, then we are fools or traitors or cowards. We do not need to be super-spiritual to be led by God. No scriptural record shows that Pilate ever prayed, yet he had a clear inkling about the innocence of Jesus. The Gospel of John records that no less than three times did Pilate voice this feeling that Jesus had "no guilt" (John 18:38; 19:4, 6). If skeptical Pilate could have an inkling, can't Christians expect the inner leading of God? Pilate took the inner leading to be nonbinding when it came time to act. "Pilate made efforts to release Him . . . He then delivered Him up to them to be crucified" (John 19:12, 16). On the other hand, when Jesus walked out of the garden from prayer, no person or circumstance could keep Him from His decision to follow His Father's leading.

Action perfects our faith, our witness, and our world. James 2:22 says, "As a result of the works, faith was perfected." The Greek word for perfected means "brought to its proper fulfillment" or "completed in its appropriate use." God is interested in developing in us a faith perfected by works. He wants our faith to grow by what we do. His desire for us is not mere behavioral change (which is what politics desires), His desire is that our faith be increased by our actions. The health of our faith is determined by exercising it. Faith not dear enough to stimulate action is dead.

Action also perfects our witness. Not only is God waiting for us to participate politically, the world is, too. Do we mean what we believe? How will the world know if we do not act upon it? Let's not be intimidated by secular people who disparage Christian involvement in politics. It is not the Christian involvement but usually the manner and the tone of Christian involvement that bothers them. Nonbelievers watch to see whether the followers of Christ will ever make a significant difference outside the walls of their churches. Recently an article in our local newspaper explained that the school board would be reviewing sex education curriculum. The paper quoted the chairperson as saying, "I hope we can get the committee organized before all the Christians start talking about morals and abstinence." That sounds like a derisive remark, and I am sure it was meant that way. Yet it is also a remark that connotes a certain respect. She was viewing the participation of Christians as certain enough and significant enough to concern her. I wonder how much her respect for Christianity would decrease if we were not interested or strong enough to give input. Our involvement is not only to do and say "what we are supposed to," it is also to give others grounds to take Christianity seriously. When Christ becomes a force to be reckoned with, He will also become a face to be recognized.

As for action perfecting the world, perhaps "perfecting" is too strong a word. Maybe "limiting destruction" or "making things better" would be more accurate. Whatever phrase is on our minds, the point is that God loves people. He loves us enough that He does not exclude government as a tool by which He can inspire us to help each other. Through our government we have the chance to influence profoundly the lives of people all over the world. No, we cannot convert them through government. Yes, their eternal salvation is most important. But that does not mean that every other provision that could be made through government is unimportant. It does not mean that the stewardship of the earth is not a concern because conversion is. Our government has certain powers, minor next to God's, but still rather potent. Our government can feed the hungry, relieve people from oppression, even model strength with integrity to the world. But without action from the Christ followers in our nation, that potential will be incomplete, unfulfilled, or morally destructive.

God will call some people to unique service in government. He has done that historically with kings such as David, vice-pharaohs such as Joseph, judges such as Samson and Deborah, queens such as Esther, and prophets such as Nathan. But how many Davids or Josephs or Nathans does God need? If He is not calling us to be the leading government official, what, then, will He call most of us to do?

1. *Become Informed.* Set your "favorites" on Websites that can keep you informed, some of them will send you email alerts or offer podcasts. Read newspapers, watch news programs, but spend time in Scripture, and read "values producing" books. The Holy Spirit can use political material to move us to take appropriate action. It is not unlike how He uses Scripture.

    The source of the reading material is important. Many evangelicals use materials that come from a clearly evangelical slant. That is fine. The liberal Christian perspective and the humanist perspective are also valuable. Newspapers usually have a section for political news (the bias varies with the paper). Some papers and Websites have summaries of how your government representatives voted that week. Information is not our enemy, but neither is it our ultimate guide. The Holy Spirit is the One who will lead us to the best personal decisions, even in the political arena.

2. *Write.* Everything we have always wanted to say to the government through our representatives is at our fingertips. Everything we want to say to our community through a letter to the editor is at our fingertips. What we may desire to say to our school board or county commissioner simply needs a mouse and a keyboard.

It may be rather intimidating for those who have never written to someone holding a governmental office before to do so. Several lists of "how to" write government officials net the following commonsense points:

   a. Spell the person's whole name correctly on the letter and envelope; use appropriate titles such as The Honorable or President when appropriate.

   b. Keep your letter brief and if you aren't using a computer, write legibly. Double-check your grammar and spelling. Or, ask someone else to do it for you.

   c. Know your subject, including the numbers of any legislative bills to which you are referring.

   d. Be specific in stating your opinion or desire.

   e. Don't threaten.

   f. Make sure the matter you are addressing falls under the jurisdiction of the person you are writing. Determine whether you should be corresponding with a local, state or federal official about your concern.

When writing to any forum, newspaper, school board, or government official, be sure to link your concern to the general public's well-being.

Also remember, public officials will be limited severely if the only input they get from their constituency is a positive or negative vote on election day. Our government policies will be limited to the perspective of our representatives if citizens never express themselves. Civil service, like any vocation, has its own parochial pattern of thinking. Conversations with other civil servants can net some new ideas and solutions, but not varied perspectives. Without the expression of ideas, questions, and problems from the citizens, a representative type of government can become every bit as isolated as a dictatorship. The isolation of our governing officials is not intentional, but it is very real.

More specifically, Christians need to write public officials about particular religiopolitical matters that concern us all. Where will these representatives find informed, spiritual input if not from us? We cannot expect nonbelievers to make godly decisions in a vacuum. Neither can we expect believing representatives to enact such decisions without our support. Civil servants need new, fresh, workable, godly input. They also might be delighted to hear that we are praying for them. Unfortunately, most of our government representatives have an image of Christians who are more ready to cut them off at the knees than to spend time on our knees for them.

3. *Vote*.

4. *Do volunteer work in politics*. Some of us are naturals for service. "Martha" personalities (as Martha is described in Luke 10:38-42) are task- and activity-oriented. This is also true of people who have the spiritual gifts of helps or service. When some issue or candidate comes their way, the response

is to do something about it. More accurately, it is to do many things about it.

Some "Marthas" will be fascinated by the activity of politics and choose to be a mainstay of the community in political activities. Balancing ministering to their families as well as their work, such contributors are a great witness to God's quiet corps. These folks have a serving ministry that sets others free to proclaim and explain (Acts 6:2-4). "Marthas" are terrific in doing necessary precinct work such as mailings, phone calling, registering people to vote, working at the polls, etc. They are the organizers of political conventions. These men and women put forth 90 percent of the effort it takes to attract voters (the other 10 percent being the "glory jobs").

Some "Marthas" will be called to one particular issue, or perhaps a few, for a limited period of time. They may have a special burden for issues concerning children, or women, or civil rights. Such a ministry is also valuable to model that short-term callings are as valid to God as lifelong volunteer careers. If our ideal is obedience, not simple human effort, then the Lord is in charge of the length of service. Many times He will use volunteer public service as a transition into another ministry.

5. *God may lead you to run for office.* Politics is honorable work. And, an evangelical in political office can be a powerful witness. With the single exception of celebrity religious leaders and the complications they would bring, evangelical officeholders can be most effective as they live their normal Christian lives without special crusades. They understand that serving the Lord will at times lead them into conflict with the culture and with government, but political office is their calling. They

witness verbally when the Lord gives them an opening, but their mission in office is not to evangelize Congress. Individual example more effectively penetrates American pluralism than does organized religious group effort.

Perhaps God is calling you to be a part of His work in politics. It is not a more holy calling than being a Christian who digs ditches and no less holy a calling than being a nationally recognized evangelist. It is simply a job for which God may have made you.

Pilate, like many of us, never really took action. He went through the normal political motions. He had some inner leading, but it did not lead him. He dispensed with his political duty as painlessly as possible, doing what seemed at the time to serve the best interests of all, except Jesus.

Imitators of Christ in politics will do the opposite of what Pilate did. When we are confronted with a political issue that has direct moral implications, we first need to be in prayer, not in motion. As with Christ, any action we take must arise from prayer. As with Christ, the action will not aim primarily at expanded worldly power or visible results. The action will be simple obedience.

If our political actions are a result of prayer, our actions will have a very different tone from other political actions. That action (participation) will be filled with tolerance and healing. It will be an invitation to something better, rather than competition with what already exists.

STEP 6: Tolerate others and encourage understanding.

There are two types of tolerance. One type of tolerance ennobles; the other type of tolerance corrupts. One type of tolerance is active; the other type of tolerance is passive. The first type of tolerance is neither afraid of nor destroyed by conflict. The second type is many times the excuse for avoiding conflict at all costs. The first tolerance is necessary for the extension of ideals and beliefs; the second downplays ideals and beliefs because they disturb the peace.

Americans and Christians have defined tolerance inaccurately. Much of what has passed for tolerance in this country has been indifference or empty-headedness. True tolerance comes in the midst of conflict. True tolerance respects and sharpens; it does not dull or ignore. True tolerance has a power to cultivate the hallmarks of both discipleship and patriotism—passion and freedom. But before we exercise true tolerance, we need to exorcise false tolerance.

Tolerance is not indifference. One is a virtue of hard work; the other is a sin of laziness. Both the nation and the Lord require of us maximum effort to effect our destiny. On the experiential level, individual participation is demanded. Passion is required. Arthur Schlesinger, Jr., writes, "Americans can take pride in their nation, not as they claim a commission from God and a sacred destiny, but as they fulfill their deepest values in an enigmatic world. America remains an experiment. Only hard work at the experiment will achieve the destiny. The outcome is by no means certain."[2] Scripture calls for the same passion in our efforts. Christ chides the people of Laodicea when He says, "I know your deeds, that you are neither cold nor hot; I wish that you were cold or hot. So because you are lukewarm, and neither hot nor cold, I will spit you out of My mouth" (Revelation 3:15-16).

Indifference that tries to pass as tolerance is not acceptable. We cannot hang our acceptance of other people's opinions over shrugged shoulders.

True tolerance requires caring and participation with the opposition. It involves healing by hearing without retreat. It involves healing by offering our side without apology, whatever the reaction. True tolerance is emotional work.

Tolerance is not only a requirement for righteous citizenship, but also the hope of our God of reconciliation. It is what He Himself exercises. Second Peter 3:9 states the reason Christ has not come again: "The Lord is not slow about His promise . . . but is patient toward you, not wishing for any to perish but for all to come to repentance." God now tolerates rebellion and wrong thinking as a provision toward reconciliation. The hope of reconciliation must also be ours. There is no hope, no understanding, and no communication without tolerance. Unfortunately, and ironically, many individuals who are the most intense about their faith are the least tolerant. The intensity-intolerance link is a stumbling block to the unbelieving world that looks for the purity of religion and love to be combined. The famous French atheist Voltaire wrote in his *Philosophical Dictionary* (1764), "Of all religions, the Christian is without doubt the one which should inspire tolerance most, although up to now Christians have been the most intolerant of men." Most individuals retain an adolescent habit: they define their existence using negatives. Like middle school children that punctuate their conversations with, "I hate school. . . . He's a jerk. . . . She is so stuck-up. . . . Don't you just hate math?" Christians are much more prone to the negative than the positive. It is easier to state what we hate than what we love.

Unfortunately, some Christian leaders have found that hate and fear are the most effective ways of raising money. People are willing to pay to be assured they are right and to be protected. The more you can polarize issues and make the other side look evil, the more funds you can raise for your organization.

Many times the more dogmatic a local church gets about its faith, or any moral issue, the more exclusive it becomes. Yet when most people, nonbelievers included, picture Jesus, they picture Him as loving, gathering, including all.

Conversely, many of the churches that are most tolerant are the least passionate about what they believe. They prize people, not only above doctrine, but almost to the ignorance of doctrine. They cannot claim spiritual maturity even if they may claim emotional maturity. Yet when most people picture Jesus, they picture Him as not compromising the truth.

In retrospect, the religious crowd of Jesus' day had passion, but insisted on denying freedom. That is intolerance. Pilate had no passion; he was detached. That is false tolerance. Jesus spoke the truth and loved without needing agreement. That is tolerance. The difference between Christians and their Lord is not one of intent, but one of maturity. We have not yet "become conformed to the image of His Son, that He might be the firstborn among many brethren" (Romans 8:29). When Christians mature to the point that our intensity and inclusiveness combine, we will be agents of true tolerance. We will be a healing presence in politics and everywhere else. There will be great breadth in our worldview while we fix our eyes upon Jesus (Hebrews 12:2). There will be a freedom in our ability to understand and a discipline in our thinking. *True tolerance is the hallmark of zeal instead of its opposite*. Passion and freedom meet in tolerance, and tolerance sets the stage for reconciliation. Jesus modeled this. Passion and freedom are hallmarks of His ongoing invitation to find the Truth.

The Pilate Process is a simple procedure for a Christian approaching politics. Procedures, unlike "expert" analyses, give us permission to advance into areas that may be new to us. Procedures keep us from using uncertainty as an excuse for not acting. The assumption in a procedure is that almost any individual is capable of doing the job, at his own pace. The advantage of this procedure is that it avoids several traditional pitfalls in political participation.

The Pilate Process emphasizes maturity in individual thinking. The best leaders need strong followers who can arrive at political decisions independently. Without some do-it-yourself emphasis, followers will be too mindless to prune leadership, and leaders will be too elevated to work for followers. Good political leaders are extremely important. We will always hope that people with special abilities and passionate vision can unify the rest of us in common interests and common effort. That is the natural way. Arthur Schlesinger, Jr., writes, "Government throughout human history has always been government by minorities—that is, by elites. This statement is as true for democratic and communistic states today as it was for medieval monarchies and primitive tribes. Masses of people are structurally incapable of directed self-government. They must delegate their power to agents."[3] Leadership is both a need and a desire for most of us.

The Pilate Process emphasizes personal performance of Scripture over public interpretation of Scripture. Christians have confused their responsibility to follow Scripture with their habit of making Scripture the agenda. Thinking, tolerance, prayer and action are Christlike.

As a procedure, The Pilate Process lessens our tendency

toward a political binge and purge syndrome. There are times when we are so consumed with the issues of the day, and feel so overloaded that we will do almost anything to get rid of the stress. A deliberating procedure helps us pace our involvement. Taking on everything limits us, but taking on certain things energizes us.

The Pilate Process makes us "GOOD AT" politics:

Get away from the confrontational demonstration — to think.

Overlook a narrow religious perspective.

Observe deep principles rather than shallow politics.

Decide from prayer and scriptural principles.

ACT!

Tolerate others and encourage understanding.

Notes

1. Robert Booth Fowler, *Religion and Politics in America* (Methuchen, N.J.: Scarecrow, 1984), 73.

2. Arthur Schlesinger, Jr., *The Cycles of American History* (Boston: Houghton Mifflin, 1986), 21-22.

3. Ibid., 428.

EIGHT
PROPER PUNCTUATION IN POLITICS:
How to Express What God Has Given Us

One word of truth outweighs the world.

— Alexander Solzhenitsyn

She was the strictest teacher I ever had. She wore her hair in a tight bun, and her feet were stuffed in what resembled combat boots. She marched up and down the aisles teaching fear and English composition … in that order. I can remember the value she attached to punctuation.

"The development of your story depends upon the correct separation of thoughts. It must be executed with the appropriate emphasis in expression. Horrible accidents can occur to communication without proper punctuation!" I pictured sentences running headlong into each other because they had no punctuation marks to stop them. Their meanings could barely be seen in the wreckage. Their beautiful little messages, so full of vibrancy and potential, were snuffed out because someone forgot the punctuation. "Even worse," she continued (I held my breath), "can you imagine the misunderstanding that comes with incorrect punctuation?" I pictured a strong proclamation unnerved by a question mark. I pictured a declaration cut to pieces by commas.

OK, so junior high boys may get weird when bored. But proper punctuation, figuratively and literally, will make or break any story. Just so, punctuation will provide the separation and emphasis needed for Christians to express themselves in politics.

My teacher knew that saying the right thing in the wrong place or at the wrong time or in the wrong way can cause problems. So we must be vigilant about the structure of what we say. We need to realize the most productive expression is one fitly spoken (Proverbs 25:11). It is the expression that is properly emphasized so that it has the maximum effect. If we could ask ourselves what kind of expression is most appropriate for our concern, we would be so much more powerful in our communication.

Four punctuation marks will serve as an example of how, if living can be aligned with writing, our expression can be sharpened. Think punctuation.

PUNCTUATION MARK #1: The Proclamation of the Exclamation Point

Some things need to be proclaimed! Warnings, surprises, and hurts are causes to lose caution. They are reasons to become, as one politician described himself, a raging moderate. Remember, exclamations are made stronger by contrast. When Jesus, on rare occasion shouted, it was a dramatic change from his normal, gentle manner of teaching. This is not so with much political and religious expression. There are some religious leaders and some political leaders who cannot talk without shouting. Their exclamations will go unheeded. People whose every cry is "Wolf!" are ignored eventually, even when there is a wolf.

But a raging moderate is a sight to behold and a sound to hear! Raging moderates realize that punctuating the equilibrium with an increase in volume only on rare occasions is an effective way to make a point that insists on making a radical difference.

Warnings need to be proclaimed! Listen to Jesus preach in Matthew 23. He is speaking out against acts that are culturally acceptable but spiritually empty. He is not teaching in a monotone. He is not simply relaying information in an objective fashion. He is pleading with people to repent, to turn around in their ways. Because of His heartfelt concern for them, He is trying to get them to change. His voice has every indication of intensity, even alarm. He uses the strongest words to provoke their full attention. And Jesus does all of this because He sees clearly the guilt that will be upon them (v. 35). He is trying to tell His nation of the consequences of their actions.

Do you see clearly the consequences of our present pattern of living? If you do, proclaim it! Send it to your government representative. Tell it to the church. Say it to your friends. Then leave it to people to decide whether or not they will listen. Maybe the warning is a call to wake up, to pay attention to the consequences that our grandchildren will face if the national moral debt continues to increase. Maybe the warning is a prophetic one, such as the consequences for a society whose main value is pleasure and main goal is retirement. If God has given you a glimpse of what is happening to us all, tell your representatives your concern!

Surprises need to be proclaimed! Blessed are those who are still shocked! The great moments of advancement in our history are those moments when we have been, as a people, appalled. From the abolitionists to the civil rights marchers, to contemporary national efforts such as Bono's ONE Campaign, Americans have not failed to respond when they "realized how bad it was." Our capacity for improvement corresponds to our ability to be repulsed or taken aback by what we see. In every Gospel, Jesus is pictured as appalled by the moneychangers in the temple (Matthew 21:12-17; Mark 11:15-18; Luke 19:45-46; John 2:13-22). They had been there for years; so had He. But He still had the capacity to be shocked by profane behavior.

Many Americans have lost their ability to be shocked. Englishman Alistair Cooke's commentary on America recorded, "I myself think I recognize here several of the symptoms that Edward Gibbon maintained were signs of the decline of Rome and which arose not from external enemies but from inside the country itself. A mounting love of show and luxury. A widening gap between the very rich and the very poor. An obsession with sex . . . exercising military might in places remote from the centers of power . . . the general desire to live off the state . . . *And, most disturbing of all, a developing moral numbness to vulgarity, violence, and the assault on the simplest human decencies*"[1] (italics mine). Nevertheless, what capacity for shock we still retain should be unleashed with exclamatory emphasis! The emphasis may be required to get a hearing. It will at least let us know we are not entirely callous.

Hurts also need to be announced! In a world of war, poverty, genocide, AIDS, child pornography, and sex slavery we should hurt for the hurting. Many Christians want to know more than they want to care. *Until we care, it does not matter how much we know.* Unless we proclaim the need for peace, healing and justice, the mission of Christ (Luke 4:18) is still a foreign mission to us.

The effort that many Christians put forth toward protecting the unborn is to be commended. Whenever the subject of harming humans arises, many Christians instinctively assume an offensive stance against abortion. And that is a good thing. We live in a society that is in many ways more sensitive to animal life than human life. Anyone who takes an egg from the nest of an officially "endangered bird" is liable to a fine of up to five thousand dollars and a sentence of up to five years in jail. Yet a fertilized human egg is not so protected. The Internal Revenue Service recognizes a cattle breeder's expenses for a calf *from the date of conception*, but our legal system will not give the same protected status to a human baby. We rightly cry out for the protection of the innocent. We rightly call out to protect the disabled from "mercy killing." But let that person be an adult who has participated in his or her own demise, and many Christians will show little compassion.

Hurt is no less hurt, tragedy is no less tragedy, because it is self-inflicted. It may be more frustrating. It is certainly more complex. But one test of maturity is the ability to be compassionate and steadfast in cases of, as Menninger wrote, *Man Against Himself.* Many of the social problems that the government and the church will be called to resolve will be those of self-destruction. When those who are hurting want help, the church is in a unique position to respond. Government can provide funds and education, but neither funds nor education can root out the problems. The church, stirred by our insistence on compassion, can provide funds, education, family support *and a life-changing experience with Christ.* The exclamation for resolutions, in this case, do not need to be pointed so much at senators as at ministers, elders, and church leaders. The church needs to say with her God, "I have surely seen the affliction of My people ... and have given heed to their cry" (Exodus 3:7).

So there is a place for an exclamation point in the Christian expression. When God speaks in your heart about warning, or surprise, or hurting, back your proclamations with facts and let them be heard!

PUNCTUATION MARK #2: The Caution of the Semicolon

The complexity of politics intimidates people. They feel a pressure to have the answer before they think issues through. Most people will either put forth no ideas, or they are pushed to the opposite extreme of needing to appear that they have the answer. Like some animals, there are people who, when intimidated, keep very still hoping not to be noticed while others blow up to look fiercer than they are. Both need to be relieved of the pressure of having all the answers before they speak. Both need to realize the value of semicolon statements. These statements only start a thought; then they are continued and refined by another thought.

Semicolon statements are begun with initial statements that immediately stimulate follow-up thoughts. The initiating thoughts are complete, but not entire. The art of making semicolon statements might lead us to our own conclusions about how to use such statements.

Christians often make conclusive political statements; we should instead make initial political statements. The former will mandate simple response; the latter will invite thinking and maturity. The former gives people the choice to submit or rebel; the latter gives people the opportunity to perfect the statement.

When a local church says, for example, "abortion is wrong," it is a complete truth by itself, but it is not the entire truth. It is an automatic response, but does not engender a full response. It is a period statement. A semicolon statement might be, "For those who believe abortion is wrong there is much work to be done; _____." The sentence expects a continuation. There are several ways to complete it, only one of which has been used by most local churches; "We must prevent it." Deeper thinking provides deeper obligations. M. Scott Peck writes in *The Different Drum*, "There are no simple solutions. Anyone who thinks with integrity on the subject will feel torn apart. On the other hand, there is no question that abortion is murder of a sort and that a policy of abortion on demand does tend to diminish what Albert Schweitzer called 'reverence for life.' On the other hand, there is no question as to the magnitude of the suffering that would result for both parents and children if abortion of the misbegotten were not an option … . To legally say 'Thou shalt not abort' is simplistic. Something is missing, left out. We cannot with integrity take responsibility away from individuals as to what they will do with their lives and pregnancies and then put it nowhere. The responsibility has to go somewhere. We cannot with integrity say 'Thou shalt not abort' unless we … are willing to assume great responsibility for the financial and psychological health of the individual and child to be."[2]

The local church that initiates with a truth about any issue should deepen the truth with follow-up concerns and assistance. The pastor or elders or proper authority in a local church will do well to speak truth for its own improvement. Semicolon statements indicate further development in ideas and people. Semicolon statements indicate that closely related concerns will follow immediately so that what is true can be entire.

An example of a semicolon statement is one between a constituent and his government representative. Many constituents write only when they are angry about an issue. If the letter exclaims an accusatory point aimed at intimidating, not informing, that is not the best message to send. But even more constituents do not write at all because they do not have an entire answer. They do not realize that they have the right to express concern without having the complete solution. The most helpful correspondence for a government representative is a semicolon statement. It has the tone of partnership. It expresses what it knows; it does not know it all. It seeks to support in return for support. It seeks to initiate, hoping for fulfillment. Note the differences in these four statements to a public official:

1. If you ignore the threat of smut, you will be responsible for turning our America into a garbage heap!
2. Can't you do anything about pornography?
3. Pornography is such a serious blight on our land that I wish you would do something about it.
4. It would give me great encouragement to think that we could stand together in support of the Commission on Pornography Report; _____.

Which would inspire you most to address the concern? Tone and expectation expressed in our correspondence do have an affect. Obviously when writing or speaking of a real concern, we would not leave a semicolon statement incomplete; the example merely illustrates the openness to partnership. One fitting conclusion might be, "I would be honored to support you in any helpful bill you might propose." There is a difference between an offering of anger, of ignorance, of opinion, and of partnership. There is a difference between loading the entire burden on government officials (washing your hands of it) and being willing to be connected with them in their efforts for us.

In addition to partnership, semicolon statements imply a steadfastness of thought. Exclamations can be short-lived. Their spokesmen can burn out or get distracted by other issues. People who tend to exclaim can do so in spurts on one subject or, in habit, on every subject. They can be difficult to count on over the long haul. The same can be true of people whose political concerns are mostly questions. If their questions are not addressed within an allotted period of time, they may get discouraged and quit. Those whose political statements are simple declarations may or may not connect them into a coherent and durable pattern of concern. But a semicolon thought, by definition, looks to be followed by another like it. Semicolon communication represents unfaltering, unswerving, purposeful thought. Like the punctuation mark, it will stand out as an irritant until it is completed (review statement four). Semicolon communication looks to be joined with ideas that develop it to maturity. Semicolon communication is not brainstorming; it is evolving improvement. As such, it is a more welcomed communication, especially in today's society.

Our society is not becoming known for its tenaciousness of thought and effort. Rose Bird, a former California chief justice, was once quoted as saying, "Ours is an amphetamine society, without the stability of an anchor, hurtling from one idea to another, momentarily clinging to them for support, but then discarding them."[3] Paul had the same problem in mind when he admonished Christians, "We are no longer to be children, tossed here and there . . . and carried about by every wind of doctrine" (Ephesians 4:14). Indeed, if we could persevere in developing a fraction of our good intentions, any portion of our good ideas, society would see the benefits of steadfastness. People would understand the value of loyalty to an ideal in contrast to the vapor of impulse.

Constituents who communicate a semicolon statement to their congressman (or pastor or board member or, even, spouse) have a much better chance of response than those who do not. Semicolon statements convey respect and trust because of the reply that is being requested.

One last example of a semicolon statement is intercessory prayer. How can we pray boldly, but not presume to order God? How can we lay our concerns about the government before God, expecting Him to finish and perfect them? We need not command God in a shout. We need not offer solutions for Him to accomplish. That is not prayer; it is arrogance. We need to look for His leading for our action. Intercessory prayer is not a flat statement to God, informing Him of the world's condition and washing our hands of the matter. No, when Scripture tells us in 1 Timothy 2:1-2 to make intercession "on behalf of all men, for kings and all who are in authority," it is urging a semicolon stance. That is, it is a positioning of ourselves between the concern we have for the world and what God will do to finish that concern. It yokes our intentions with God's extension. It offers our beginning understanding to His completing response.

Books have been written on the dynamic of intercessory prayer; I speak only to its basic attitude. Whether the prayer is for politics or people, the real intercessor is not just a voice of concern, he is an intermediary looking to be stretched. The goal of the semicolon punctuation mark is to connect and to extend. The goal in religion and politics is to both connect us and extend our thinking.

Semicolon types of communication can be used when the objective is not to stand alone but to team up, and when the objective is not to make the point but to make a start. Some more examples, contrasted with other types of punctuation, may help:

Being a sinner means you'd better turn or burn! vs. I asked Christ to make a difference in my life; _____.

What can be done about crime? vs. I have a beginning idea that could make a dent in our crime problem; _____.

God, I really think my son is one of your mistakes. vs. Lord, I want to stand with You and my son; _____.

There are many different ways those sentences could be completed, but in every case the initiate is involved in the completion. There are times to stand toe to toe against some legislation, court decision, or sin. In those times it is fitting to declare opposition and to strategize what corrective measures can be taken. But many more times our participation calls for us to be linked and stretched by working to perfect or better the efforts already underway.

Semicolons symbolize the best relationship between politics and religion. Church and state are institutions that should not be mixed. But in matters of religion and politics, a semipermeable membrane is appropriate. That is, politics must not be separated from religious values; religion must not be separated from political responsibility. One matures and completes the other; the connection must be close. Certainly politics and religion become more distinct and less diluted, with some separation. The semicolon motif is a perfect connecting divider for religiopolitical dialogue.

PUNCTUATION MARK #3: The Quest of the Question Mark

Questions can be used simply to obtain information, and they should be. But questions have a larger use in political expression. They can be used to provoke thinking and change. Unlike semicolon expression, in which the initiate is linked to the response, questions taken seriously can cause reactions in others.

Admittedly, many questions used in politics and religion are fake. Much of the time they are, like Pilate's "What is truth?" not really questions at all. They are mere rhetorical points scored in verbal battle. A real question should mark a real search in religion or politics. A probing question can cause a reaction that may be as valuable as the answer. A probing question is a catalyst.

Carl Archdeacon taught me about catalysts; he could teach us all. Anyone traveling through Shelby, Ohio, in the early 1960s could have looked at Mr. Archdeacon and said, "That man is a chemistry teacher." They would have been correct.

Mr. Archdeacon stood behind the counter one afternoon. He was teaching from his usual spot, looking his usual self. His hair was parted down the middle, years after and years before that part was in style. His glasses kept creeping down his nose, and he would take his hand off his slide rule just long enough to push them back up. His bow tie divided his faultless mind from his rolled-up white sleeves. And he droned on as I did my usual math research: counting holes in the ceiling tile (I had already counted the blocks in the wall and the pens in his shirt). But this day my math projects would be interrupted. I was stirred, for some reason, by an explanation of a catalyst.

"A catalyst," he said, "is a substance by which a chemical reaction is initiated or accelerated, while the catalyst itself remains unchanged." He went on with examples of an agent that would affect those elements around it but would not itself be changed.

As I began my studies in American history at Ohio University, I noticed that most of the questions asked by the history makers of our country were not just information-gathering questions. The questions were more like catalysts, stimulating an action rather than just an answer.

The famous speech of Patrick Henry in 1775 included catalytic questions such as, "Is life so dear or peace so sweet as to be purchased at the price of chains?" That question, followed by his own independent exclamation, "I know not what course others may take, but as for me, give me liberty or give me death!" stirred people to decision and action.

In the Constitutional Convention of 1787, debate continued for over a month without progress. Benjamin Franklin addressed President Washington to ask the delegates catalytic questions: "In this situation of this Assembly, groping as it were in the dark to find political truth, and scarce able to distinguish it when presented to us, how has it happened, Sir, that we have not hitherto once thought of humbly applying to the Father of lights to illuminate our understandings?" After reviewing the historic importance of prayer in our nation's break with Great Britain, he continued, "And have we forgotten that powerful Friend? Or do we imagine that we no longer need His assistance? ... God governs in the affairs of men. And if a sparrow cannot fall to the ground without His notice, is it probable that an empire can rise without His aid?" Franklin went on to propose prayer at the beginning of each session. His questions were posed to cause decision and action.

As I grew in Christ, I noticed that many of the questions in Scripture were posed to cause change as much as they were to gather information. God's questions of a sinful man and woman, when examined closely, are catalytic. When God asks, "Where are you?" of man in sin (Genesis 3:9), the question is not one of geography but of biography. The objective is for Adam to change, not for God to increase His store of information. When God asks woman in sin, "What is this you have done?" (v. 13), we must presume He already knows the answer. The objective is to cause her to come to a realization and change. In these cases and others, the information asked for was secondary to the hoped-for reaction. Catalytic questions are real questions, but the answers are not simple. They are deep and moving. Christians can ask great, stirring questions.

Questions can be used in politics and religion in the most profound, influential ways, or toward the most limited, self-serving ends. Questions can cause us to see and act in new ways, or they can be used to manipulate us without our insight. Some questions are not questions at all, but statements in disguise. They are designed to lead us to predesignated answers, giving us the impression that we reached the conclusions on our own. Really, the answers depend upon our *not* thinking.

Such questions are devices. They play upon our emotions, preventing our thinking of anything but the question. They are a sham and a shame. I heard an evangelist once tell about a man who refused to accept Christ and, "that very afternoon his little girl was run over by a car. Do you think that man did not cause his little girl's death?" The question was not asked so that we could explore theological possibilities, or even to examine the character of God. The repulsive question was asked to scare people into a yes answer to his coming altar call.

In like manner, politicians will use inflammatory questions to limit thought and exploration. The question "Do we want the terrorists to take control?" is an almost universal excuse for military action, but it does not stimulate more than one possible answer. The type of question that limits us to one possible answer while threatening us is not a catalyst; it is a cattle prod.

We have greater possibilities. The questions we ask can generate more than simple answers, sometimes without obtaining any specific answers at all. Serious questions can stimulate change and commitment. Serious questions can summon values and insight. Let us look at some of the questions Jesus asked, to use them as models.

There were question for believers: "Why are you so timid? How is it that you have no faith?" (Mark 4:40). The questions were asked of them when they were afraid of being overwhelmed by threatening forces. It had not occurred to them that they had any power over the situation. But the questions posed by Jesus were never answered directly. Instead, they were catalysts for a deeper question: "Who then is this, that even the wind and sea obey Him?" (v. 41). Evidently, the more they looked inside themselves, the more they wanted to know about Christ's power.

The questions are appropriate today, especially in the church. Why are we so timid? How is it that we have no faith? Questions like that are needed to reveal our sense of powerlessness and fear. If we listen to the news daily and read the headlines, we may feel overwhelmed. We may feel powerless to make any difference at all, but the real question is not one of power, it is one of faith. The investigation is not so much into human potential as it is into who God is in this situation. And why aren't we directly calling on Him, for either guidance or divine intervention or insight? The *why* from questions like that hardly ever result in a specific answer. Yet it is a catalyst that will activate us into a new boldness with God and His power in the world.

Jesus' question "Why does this generation seek for a sign?" (Mark 8:12) is a catalyst to change our focus from what is outward and circumstantial to what is inward and responsible. We don't want to depend on political solutions more than spiritual ones.

In our quest for the physical (usually monetary) things, our culture needs to have questions posed like, "What are the spiritual opportunities that will make a more profound difference in our lives than anything physical? Then what is really important?" Such questions are an antidote to shallowness.

Some questions can be answered, but not left at the answer. The answer is a command for further action. It is a catalyst that prompts change all around it, while remaining separated (holy) from change itself. The answer is more influential than informational. Thus, the question is a most valuable one.

Questions, then, are very useful in punctuating religiopolitical expression. The catalyst type of question, even more than the facts type of question, serves to stimulate change. We need to ask heavenly-minded Christians questions that might jar them from a spectator approach to faith. "Why do you stand looking into heaven?" (Acts 1:11) is a valid question still today. Christians must pay attention to their responsibilities in this world. We need to ask questions that will make people think through relevant opinions and evidence and then call for a firm stand. When Jesus asked the question "Who [what] do people say ... who [what] do you say ... ?" (Matthew 16:13,15), He was prompting Peter to take a stand.

Catalytic questions are always relevant. They prevent a mindless, run-on faith, making us stop and think. It is our job to ask them, listening for an answer and, even more, planting an influence. Who else will do it?

PUNCTUATION MARK #4: The Power of the Period

All three types of political expression that have just been discussed look for a response. An exclamation point attracts attention to emergency issues. A semicolon looks for some sort of development of the thought it has initiated. A catalytic question hopes for a reaction, but even more it hopes for an answer that will change the inner chemistry of our political solutions. That objective may fail. Catalytic questions take a risk. Intended to reflect righteous efforts to change the world, there is still the very real possibility that they will elicit no immediate response. Any type of political expression by Christians is, in one sense, at the mercy of cultural receptivity. When the culture responds to our expressions with silence, or "No," the effort we put into them and our emotional investment may appear to be wasted. That is one reason why Christian political expression has been sporadic throughout American history.

Christians require a certain amount of success, or at least response, for their efforts, or they get discouraged and confine their religious expressions to church. That is also why political expression must be a matter of obedience instead of courage or hope. Obedience is consistent no matter what the response; courage and hope sometimes flag when the winds of response stop. So it is that these obedient expressions toward attention, development, or reaction may appear to fail in one sense and leave their authors discouraged. There is, however, one more type of political expression that is not so dependent.

Many of us look for strong, orthodox rules of thumb in the political realm. We desire some statements that do not need to be corrected or retracted. We respect truths that cannot be swept aside or ignored. Short-term political answers, no matter how strong, do not fit into this category. Instead, statements of historical perspective and truth can provide the strong leadership compass we all need. Think long term.

Statements are expressions that need no response. By statements I mean foundational truths that summarize what our Author has said in His Word. Statements do not need to use Scripture to endorse a greater point; statements are the truths woven throughout Scripture. They are truths "we hold to be self-evident." Statements need no hype, for they are themselves a source of encouragement. Statements remind us of God's fundamental structure of the world, so that our attempts at political solutions have both proper perspective and utilitarian value. Two seem especially relevant here: individual maturity and the sovereignty of God.

Individual Maturity Is Key

We need to declare the tremendous importance of individual maturity in Christian political involvement. Scripture and experience are witness to one conclusion: there is neither a political solution nor a political system that is adequate in all circumstances and times. Rather, the key is the mature individual, or group of them, who can fit a solution or system to the common good. Telling people what to think is not as valuable as teaching them how to personally arrive at the truth.

Christianity has a unique view of the importance of individuality. Christianity differs from Eastern religions in the attention given to individuality. The goal in Eastern religions is to escape this world and eliminate the self. The goal of Christianity is to take care of this world and purify the self for the eternal dwelling with God. Christianity is also distinct from Judaism in the amount of attention given to the individual's development as differentiated from the development of a holy nation. The holy nation concern is still present in the New Testament, but there is less of a herd instinct insinuated. Instead, the holy nation is formed by individual commitment (Luke 3:8) and individual obedience empowered by the endowment of the individual with the Holy Spirit (Acts 2:38). The unity comes from the Spirit (Ephesians 4:3) instead of human agreement about goals, or political systems that unite "under God." So the holy nation is a result of individual holiness and not the cause of it. And the group cannot take the responsibility given to the individual away without crippling the group.

In many ways, the democracy of the United States reflects many of the same concerns as Christianity. Its attention to the rights of individuals, and its dependence upon the input of individuals, implies its understanding of the centrality of the individual. That has been both its strength and its weakness, for the American system is devised to accommodate individuals, not to mature them. So it is that the immaturity of Americans who expect a great government without building one may render our democracy impotent.

Group policy may be a reflection of the maturity of the individuals who composed it, but it can never be a replacement for the maturity of the individuals who live under it. The bane of our country and our Christianity is that we respect the wisdom of the Founding Fathers so much that we desire to idolize it instead of emulate it. Which of our Founding Fathers did not pay his "pound of flesh" to improve this country, and, having rid himself of that much flesh, was not enlarged in spirit? Which of the apostles, in struggling with group issues (see Acts 10 and 11), did not mature by wrestling with group policy? Somehow, we must communicate that the group arena is a training ground for individual responsibility and maturity. The goal is not the "right policy," set by a Herculean effort followed by a Rip van Winkle rest. The goal is to allow the individual to consistently address group needs as well as his own and to mature in this earthly journey because of it. Let us strive for the following balance.

Christians in politics need to know the importance of promoting individual spiritual maturity above group political fixes. We need to acknowledge that public policy has only secondhand impact upon the lives of individuals. It does not give inner direction on how to live; it is a boundary in which to live. "Christian public policy," where it has existed, has not been a cure. While its guidelines do make some positive difference to oppressed groups, the policies typically offer more comfort than aid. The main power of Christian public policy is in its ability to encourage rather than to mature. And its dangerous weakness is that the "right policy" can become a pernicious substitute, in that it is seen as a replacement for the real cure—Jesus Christ in an individual's life. Thus, if we would do people the most good, we cannot depend on group policy. Like my old pastor Dr. Shoemaker once said, "Nothing will ever come right in the world until you face the sin in your own heart."

No matter what the public policies are, the Christian's work will not be changed. There is no real improvement in society without individual spiritual development. Our goal is to equip individuals to be Christlike servants. If some government decision happens to be "pro-Christian," it could make our work a little easier. If, instead, it is "anti-Christian," it could make our work a little more difficult. But the goal of our work remains the same. We will always focus on helping individuals benefit the community. That focus is not radically affected by public policy.

The extension of our building of servants is a key in our addressing public policy. Having recognized the importance of personal development that benefits the community, we must also recognize the importance of individual responsibility toward the government. The government may have only a secondhand impact on our lives, but that is still a significant impact.

We care about public policy for two very important reasons: because we care about individuals as a whole (James 2:15-16) and secondly we can't completely love our neighbor without addressing the government that affects him because God has given each of us a responsibility in taking care of His world (Mark 13:34).

What part of a person's life is the spiritual part? I cannot find any dividing line in a human life. Every influence upon an individual chisels one more mark on his character. Maturity comprehends the complex interaction of the various influences and cares about them all. Maturity does what it can toward the person's environment, as well as toward the person himself, as an act of love. That includes addressing government policy. Such group focus must always be the minor and not the major part of our efforts, unless we have been called to a ministry of public service. But, in all cases, government is important for the sake of individuals and our ministry to them.

Also, stewardship of this world is not a choice, it is an order (Genesis 2:15). God does not give us all the same responsibilities, but part of our maturing is the addressing of His direct orders, in teamwork, for the care of His world until He returns. "It is like a man, away on a journey, who upon leaving his house and putting his slaves in charge, assigning to each one his task, also commanded the doorkeeper to stay on the alert" (Mark 13:34).

Maturity knows this is not my nation, not my world, just my responsibility. And maturity knows He's coming back.

The development of individual maturity cannot come in fantasies of group fixes or in limitations to "spiritual work" only. To help individuals mature, we must promote their participation in political activity. When we address politics, individual maturity is both the requirement and the goal.

God Is Sovereign

Christianity also has a unique view of history. God in Christ stands at the end of every individual's earthly life. God in Christ also stands at the end of history in general. No matter what one's particular eschatology may be, not many Christians would dispute these two facts disclosed in Scripture. It is because of these two facts, woven throughout Scripture, that we can assume that the end is woven throughout the present. God designed history for a purpose and is active in history. The participation of God in history is clear from the Incarnation (John 1:14). The development of history is clear from such concepts as His acting in the ripeness of time (Galatians 4:4). Therefore, we are not orphans, and the events of this world are not removed from the God "who works all things after the counsel of His will" (Ephesians 1:11).

We can clearly state to the world that God is in control. That puts the correct perspective on history. The Eastern religions' cyclical view of history, one in which individuals hope to cycle into nothingness, is antithetical to the Judeo-Christian view. Our firm faith, made upon the authority of Scripture, is that God uses the events of this world to develop individuals and history toward His purposes. When we understand that, politics acquires a different meaning. He uses our efforts, no matter how minimal they seem.

Politics, for Christians, is meant to be a test instead of a temptation. A test is a vehicle used for perfecting us and, hopefully, God's world (James 1:2-4). Tests are difficult, by nature, yet extremely useful in showing us both what we have and have not mastered. Our reactions to the world will manifest Christ to the extent we obey Him and to the extent we expect Him to come in history. Peter writes in a letter to those in the midst of political persecution, "Beloved, do not be surprised at the fiery ordeal among you, which comes upon you for your testing, as though some strange thing were happening to you; but to the degree that you share the sufferings of Christ, keep on rejoicing; so that also at the revelation of His glory, you may rejoice with exultation" (1 Peter 4:12-13). Our temptation is to ignore political progress or to cling to it. Our test is to share Christ's ministry even in politics, realizing that the resultant policy is not outside God's historical plan.

"Then," you say, "the outcome of the world doesn't really matter. It is just individual perfection that we are after." No, God is working in all of history to bring it to Himself (2 Peter 3:9). He is able in time to bring victory out of defeat, and He will be victorious.

Sometimes that is rather difficult to believe. Political power looks so attractive, and those who have it look so strong. Christians tend to feel deflated when they are politically defeated. But the God who used the cross for victory can use any weakness for power. A man once told me to take a serious look at history for a simple illustration of God's sovereign power.

"If I could take you back in time," he said, "to Rome, about A.D. 60, you might stand in a street and see two buildings. One would be a prison; inside would be a dark, damp cell holding one little man with a physical deformity. His name: Paul. He would be writing his testamentary letters to the church at Philippi and to his friend Philemon. When his eyes got tired, he might try to tell the prison guard about this Jesus, the Christ, who had changed his life. Rebuffed, he might sit to write again, knowing he would not give up on that guard.

"If you would look across the street, you would see the most glorious sight—the Coliseum. It would be filled with hundreds and hundreds of Rome's best citizens, all waiting for one man to enter. That man would be the ruler of the most powerful empire the world had ever seen. When that one man entered, all would stand to salute in a thunderous roar, 'Hail Caesar! Hail Caesar!'

"If you were asked to choose the more powerful man then, to which side of the street would you turn? Yet, thousands of years later, people in the mightiest country in the world are naming their children Paul and their dogs Caesar."

Above all the work we have yet to do, underneath all the expressions toward political progress we have yet to make, we need to know that individual maturity and God's sovereignty are, in the end, unbeatable. Period.

Notes

1. Alistair Cooke, *Alistair Cooke's America* (New York: Knopf, 1973), 387.
2. M. Scott Peck, *The Different Drum: Community Making and Peace* (New York: Simon and Schuster, 1987), 247.
3. *U.S. News & World Report*, 13 July 1987, 13.

NINE

ASK DR. HUNTER:

40 Frequently Asked Questions About Religion and Politics

1. Let's start with a question that gets to the heart of the matter: Is America a Christian nation?

To paraphrase Forrest Gump in his movie: "Stupid is as stupid does.'" Well, Christian is as Christian does. So on that basis, the answer is no. America is mostly a secular nation. While 80 percent of Americans claim to be at least nominally Christian, most of us aren't living like followers of Christ. We do have in our history an abundance of references to Scripture and to Christianity in our important government papers. But though it was mostly Christians that founded and shaped our history, several of the most influential founding fathers were deists.

We have strayed from any Christian foundation. We may be the most church-going nation in the world, but the culture itself is not "Christian" by any stretch of the imagination.

2. What was the founding fathers' intent with regards to church and state?

Ironically, the intent was originally not to impose a religion on people. Article 1 of the amendments to the Constitution says this, "Congress should make no law respecting an establishment of religion or prohibiting the free exercise thereof." So it was mostly to keep the state out of the church's business instead of keeping the Christians out of the state's business. We must remember that the founding fathers thought in terms of institutions, not in terms of individuals. They would have thought nothing about how religious an individual was who became involved in government. Personal reasons for becoming involved in politics would not have been given any consideration. So when they talked about church and state, it was mostly to protect the church from the state, not the state from the individuals in the church. The "wall" separating the institutions of church and state that Jefferson referred to only in a personal letter had little to do with the founding fathers' thoughts about interaction between government and Christians.

3. Where should we draw the line between church and state? Should there even be a "line" at all?

Yes. There should be a line when you're talking about institutions. The church as an institution can only prosper spiritually if its power is in persuasion or influence; the state's power comes from force. The church as an institution may be tempted to turn to the state and use its force to further the church's goals. There should be a line between any institutional doctrine and the force of the state. But there should never be a line between Christians and the state.

4. Aren't faith, and our political beliefs, private affairs? Why should a Christian political view be expressed in public at all?

Jesus says in Acts 1:8, "You shall be My witnesses both in Jerusalem, and in all Judea and Samaria, and even to the remotest part of the earth." Our job while we're still on earth is to make our faith public so that others can also come to know and believe in the Lord of peace, the Lord of grace, Jesus Christ. Christians should be demonstrating the Gospel in all areas of life. We should have the same words and deeds in everyday life that we have in church. So the bottom line is this: We are what we believe. We need to be able to live and speak what we believe. Should we keep quiet in public because we might offend someone? Not unless we want to be hypocrites.

5. Does the Bible say anything about churches being involved in politics?

No, not much. The instruction for churches mostly centers on how to conduct the business of churches. In 1 Timothy 2:1-2, Paul writes, "I urge that entreaties and prayers, petitions and thanksgivings, be made on behalf of all men, for kings and all who are in authority, so that we may lead a tranquil and quiet life in all godliness and dignity." It does mention honoring all men, especially the king, but it doesn't say much about churches and politics, per se.

6. Should Christians panic when ungodly people are elected into office?

Of course not! First of all, our system is set up with checks and balances. Even the tremendously powerful person, or policy, in our system will be counterbalanced by some other offsetting voice or branch. Second—and this is especially true for moral decisions and moral issues—every time something really bad happens, it causes a really big reaction. That's a good thing! So if you get somebody in office who's a moral moron (sorry to use that term, but it's appropriate) that will evoke all sorts of Christian reaction. People are going to be involved in politics who have never been involved in politics before!

Third, we don't need to panic because God is sovereign. He has promised that He will make all things work together for good to those who love Him and are called according to His purpose

(Romans 8:28). That's not just a nice theory, it works in real life. When things look their worst, don't panic; God will flip the situation around and use it for good.

7. Does government have the right to "legislate morality"?

Actually, the government does little else. Every policy the government makes has an underlying moral value. Legislation is passed, decisions are made because it thinks it's the right thing to do. So the question isn't really can you legislate morality, it's whose morality do you legislate? And if there aren't Christians offering their understanding of morality, if they abdicate, there won't simply be a vacuum. There will be other people, from a more secular standpoint or from other value bases, who will offer their understanding. So legislating morality is not the concern. It's which morality will get legislated.

8. Should a pastor dictate to his congregation how to vote?

The short answer to that is no, not unless he wants to keep his congregation in a perpetual childlike state. Members of the congregation need a personal understanding of what's right and what's wrong. Each congregant needs to listen to the Holy Spirit, and then vote according to his or her own conscience. That is a requirement of maturity. What a pastor does need to do is make sure that he is preaching from Scripture on biblical and moral values so that those values can be applied to any particular policy or issue that comes up. That way, a pastor doesn't have to say, "OK, now this week, we're for Bill 521." Christians can decide for themselves how God would want them to come down on any issue. When a pastor trains the congregation biblically, he won't need to tell them how to vote.

9. What can a pastor legally discuss in the church with regards to politics without risking 501c3 status? Most pastors and the general public are fuzzy on this point.

They're not only fuzzy, they're petrified that somehow the government's going to come down on them. First of all, let me say this: In all of the history of our country, not one of those tax exemptions has ever been taken away (except for one church, and that was only for a short period of time). You have to do something extraordinarily stupid to even have your tax status questioned!

Churches have many more rights than you would think. And if you want to know those more specifically, visit Liberty Council online (www.lc.org). This organization will tell you all of the rights that pastors and churches have and don't have. And, they'll give you guidelines. Stick by those and you'll be fine.

10. Is there a danger that evangelicals have become captive to the GOP (the Republican Party)?

If we are speaking of the white evangelical vote, the answer to that is absolutely yes! It's well known in political circles that the GOP almost takes the evangelical vote for granted. And the Democratic Party has nearly given up on the evangelical vote, which is really sad. If evangelicals don't want to be taken for granted, we really need to broaden our venue and our issues. But when you're taken for granted by one party and ignored by the other, your influence becomes pretty marginalized. Being able to have some influence on only one party is a weak position. So we're not in a really great place right now. But we're in a great place to change.

11. Do leaders within the religious right, both past and present, speak for God?

I hope not! No leader speaks for God except when he speaks straight from Scripture. Even then, the Scripture being quoted is only part of God's larger Word. The traditional leaders of the religious right have narrowed their focus to just a few issues. Those issues are biblically based, but some Christian leaders' commentary on them has gotten out of bounds. So no, they don't speak for God.

12. Why is Protestant religious faith so closely associated with the so-called "religious right"? Is there a "Christian left"?

First of all, the Protestant faith, per se, is only closely associated with the religious right because the largest part of the Protestant religious faith are evangelicals. And, evangelicals tend to be the more conservative, and the more outspoken. That is why Protestantism might be associated with the religious right.

Is there a Christian left? Absolutely. There's a whole spectrum of Christians involved in the political world. First of all, there are brilliant evangelicals whom I really admire: Jim Wallis with Sojourners; Ron Sider with Evangelicals for Social Action. These are tremendous men. The far left includes the National Council of Churches, and they are for very liberal causes. And the left, of course, would be identified more with the Democratic Party and the right more with the Republican Party. Even though we don't agree on all issues, all of us play an important role in the process.

13. Is it possible to be a believing evangelical and vote Democratic?

It's not only possible, at times, it's advisable. Let me tell you why. There are some issues that are traditionally embraced by the

Democrats that are very important biblically—issues centered around poverty, injustice, and creation care have been addressed more by the Democratic Party than by the Republican Party. Now, the compassionate conservatism of the Republican Party is catching up, and they're starting to address some of these concerns. But if you're going issue by issue, you go by the Bible … not by the party.

14. Can a person truly be a Christian if he votes for a liberal candidate?

The answer is yes. Christians are people who have acknowledged Jesus Christ as their Lord and Savior (Romans 10:9). But now, to address the point about voting for a liberal. If you know that a candidate—even though they're a liberal candidate—is a person of high integrity, and they stand with you on a lot of issues, and they're not going to negatively impact important issues (e.g. pro-life issues), or, they're simply not in a position in the government where they will impact these issues, then absolutely. You could vote for a liberal candidate for the causes that you want to see accomplished.

15. What can be done to re-brand the Christian voice in the political arena?

First of all, we need to lower the decibel level because Christians have this image of just being raving lunatics; and in some respects, it's well-deserved because people don't usually get active unless they're mad. But that's just not a good way to do politics.

Second, we need to take the attention off of issues and put it back onto moral values because moral values are much more basic. They're less yell-able. They're more to the point. They care more for people. They don't make us into enemies. They're positive.

The third thing that we have to do is expand the variety of the issues that we address. There ought to be more than just gay marriage and pro-life issues because the Bible is concerned with all of life. (By the way, the Bible is very pro-life after birth as well as before. It's concerned with how well people are taken care of, especially the vulnerable.)

The fourth thing we need to do is treat people with respect. Most people are trying to do the best they know how. And they may disagree with us, but we Christians ought to be known for our respect. The Bible says honor all men (1 Peter 2:17). We ought to honor all men.

16. Isn't a candidate's position on pro-life issues the most important thing for Christians to consider before voting?

I would say yes. Life is a prerequisite for anything else. And so if we don't protect life, then all the rest really doesn't count for much. But it's not the only important issue.

17. Is it possible to be a politician and truly be a Christian at the same time?

Yes, it is definitely possible to be a Christian and a politician because Christians get called into public service; they want to help people by serving in government. And we want them there! When the Apostle Paul was going through the Roman judicial system in Acts, he was witnessing to politicians the whole time, hoping to bring them to Christ. So, we want Christians in politics.

18. What can the Christian community do to promote bipartisan cooperation?

The key is to focus on Jesus and how He sees people. The

problem with partisanship is that we're looking at the party instead of the person. The whole problem with competition instead of cooperation is that we're looking at the issues instead of the people. One of the things that we have to do is say: How do we want this community to look? Can this person contribute to that community? How do we want this nation to look? Does this person have something to contribute to our nation? Is there a way we can help him/her contribute?

If we focus on the big picture, and get to know people's hearts, then we will have increased cooperation across party lines that we wouldn't have if we only talk about divisive issues or the differences between the ways we see things.

19. What is a proper Christian response to "right to life" issues, such as the death penalty, abortion, and doctor-assisted suicide?

The really simple answer is that we are to protect those who cannot protect themselves. And it would be startling for most people to hear me say this, but I think that is even appropriate for the death penalty. The state has a right to kill, but it is not the job of a Christian to kill what is defenseless. It is not our job to end life. It is our job to do everything we can to protect the life that is vulnerable and let God do the rest. Now, these are very complicated issues. Therefore, thinking Christians are going to disagree on these issues, particularly when it gets into what's possible medically and technically and so on. But the principle we always come back to is this: It is our job to protect life, especially when that life can't protect itself.

20. Does there ever come a time when evangelicals may have

to cast a vote for a candidate who may be more competent than Christian? If so, how should they make that decision?

The answer is yes. A wise man with good values is more effective than an incompetent Christian. I hate to be so blunt, but it's absolutely true. Some Christians have no idea what they're doing. Politics takes a certain amount of skill. When we choose a doctor, we don't want to make our decision entirely on the basis of whether or not he or she is a Christian. We want the most skilled person we can get to address the clinical problem. Likewise in choosing our political representatives. Having said that though, let me add that we certainly don't ever want to vote for someone who is immoral or who disagrees with our deepest values. If a non-Christian candidate holds many of our same values and will be much more effective than the Christian candidate, then, in all good conscience and for the good of everybody, let's cast our votes for that candidate.

Some other things that can help us decide what candidate we will support include knowing who is backing him politically and researching the candidate's public and personal efforts. Jesus said, "The very works that I do, bear witness of Me" (John 5:36). All of a person's works, not just the presence or absence of religious talk, give us a more complete picture of him and hints as to how God might use him in office.

21. When is it legitimate for a Christian to defy the government?

The only times in the Scripture that indicate it's legitimate for a Christian to defy the government are when that government is forcing him or her to do something against God's command. Civil disobedience is for a moral demonstration rather than for a political one. Therefore, we defy the government if we can't do anything else and still do what's biblically right. But we should try to think of other ways to make an impact on the government politically. Civil disobedience is about morality, not about political power, biblically speaking.

22. Is the American ideal of "Life, liberty and the pursuit of happiness" humanistic and in conflict with being a disciple of Christ?

No, but it doesn't substitute for the fullness of Christianity. Life is a good thing. Liberty is a good thing. And the pursuit of happiness is a good thing. But all of them are simply means to finding the most fulfilling relationship of all, and that is the one with Jesus Christ. And so, they're not fit goals, but they are fit means.

23. Shouldn't we just focus on preaching the Gospel and not worry about man-made political systems?

Not if we want to completely follow Christ's command to love our neighbors. Part of loving our neighbors is not just serving them personally but also paying attention to the social policy that so deeply affects their lives. Anytime we're talking about personal service, that's a compassion project. Anytime we're talking about a healthy environment for people, that takes social reform. So if we want to minister to people in a group, we're going to have to address the political system in which they live.

24. How far should we take Christ's instruction to render unto Caesar what is Caesar's? For example, if the government is using tax dollars to fund and or promote things that are ungodly, does this instruction still pertain to us?

The government's use of our taxes is about our political activity, not about our financial obligation. That is to say, we don't have the right to withhold our taxes because they're using our taxes wrongly. We have the right, politically, to reform how they use our taxes. But we don't have the right to withhold our taxes just because we don't like the way they're spending it.

25. Isn't it unbiblical for the government to have any say in what the church does, including where we build churches and what we do with the money donated?

No, it's not unbiblical because the churches are a part of society. Romans 13 says we need to obey the law, that God has put those magistrates here for a purpose: for the protection of a whole society. If we want to participate in a certain activity that's not allowed by our 501c3, we can give up our tax status if we believe that strongly in it. But the point is that the government sets up certain regulations, and Christians need to respect their neighbors and not just do what's good for their own group, but also what's good for their neighbors. That kind of deference will further their witness for Jesus Christ and make them more humble, considering others even more than they consider themselves.

26. Should all churches in America have the American flag displayed in worship?

We should display the American flag if the congregations know theologically why it is there. Christians have a dual citizenship. We are citizens of a country and citizens of Heaven (Philippians 3:20). We owe a loyalty to both homelands (Matthew 22:21). We don't want to create a civil religion. We're not worshiping

America. We're grateful to live in a nation that allows us to worship as we want, but an American flag along with a Christian flag in a church would be a great symbol of our dual citizenship.

Yet it is not a major issue and should be up to the discretion of the congregational leaders.

27. Do faith-based initiatives violate church-state separation?

Not unless you use the tax money to overtly convert people to your particular religion. What it really does is it allows the church and the state to work together to benefit the whole of society in two different ways. The state can help financially, but the church helps personally, and so it's a really good combination. Churches can help and support people to get "back on their feet" through relationships in ways government programs never can.

28. Is it wrong for churches to accept money from the government?

No. If they can use it effectively and assist people personally, then it's just a great use of tax dollars. If the government says that you can't breathe the name of Christ or somehow you've got to cover up all the crosses in your building, then the government is making you do something that isn't right. But if there are ways that you can use that money to benefit the lives of people and to love people and to help people, then that's a great use of money. You just have to watch that you're not somehow denying Christ.

29. What's a biblical response to gay marriage?

Well, when Jesus talked about marriage, He went back to the ideal in Genesis. When He was talking about divorce and men's weaknesses, He said, "It has not been so from the beginning" (Matthew 19:8). And then He talked about a man taking a wife and the two becoming one. That is the ideal we always aim for.

Now, there are two major problems for Christians in the gay marriage issue. One is this: Is it up to man to redefine marriage? Societies have the civil right to do that, but Christians don't. So Christians always need to go with the biblical definition of marriage and stand up for the biblical definition of marriage, which is between one man and one woman, as evidenced in Jesus' ideal. That would be the ideal biblical marriage.

The other problem, though, is how can you best love people who don't fit into your moral paradigm? How can you best respect them? But that's an altogether different issue than a Christian redefining marriage, which we really don't have the biblical right to do.

30. How should we respond to the removal of religious symbols from society, such as manger scenes and the Ten Commandments in courtrooms?

It should be viewed as a reproach on the ineffectiveness of Christians, rather than an attack on Christianity. We live in a secular society, and so many of the loudest voices are the most afraid of organized religion because they feel most condemned by it. And that really is a reproach on us, isn't it? Because if Christians were loving people and really making a huge difference in this society, nobody would mind our displaying the 10 Commandments or manger scenes at Christmas time. As a matter of fact, they'd be reminded that there is a group of people who are really improving the society. So this is not about our rights. This is about our ineffectiveness and our really poor witness.

31. Why do conservative Christians ignore most social issues besides abortion and homosexual rights?

These tend to be the issues that Christians want to focus on no matter what. Abortion is one of those issues; homosexuality is another. Somebody once said, "Conservative Christians seem to be focused below the belt." And I always thought that was an interesting phrase. The answer is this: If you just want to get fired up on hot-button issues, these will be the hot-button issues. But if all of life is important to you, then you have to really extend yourself to non-sex related issues.

32. Is there a place for an international effort toward a unified Christian voice, especially in emerging democracies? What would a grassroots movement of that kind look like?

Yes! I have heard from many Christians in other countries who want to address the public policy of their respective nations. "Rendering unto Caesar" implies that even if the details of being a Christian citizen vary from nation to nation, the principle biblical requirement for being one does not. So, local churches must be able to equip their congregations with ongoing guidance and support for effective political involvement, in their own country's government.

Christians in every nation are to respond to their government in ways that increase the witness of the Gospel throughout their society. That may mean building up their communities or helping to shape social policy. As the church reconnects globally for mission and evangelism, equipping the individual to be involved politically should be one of our goals together.

33. How biblical is the "Just War" theory? What would Jesus have to say about a nation taking preemptive military action?

This is a very complicated theory. There are eight rules for a "just war" as expounded on by St. Ambrose and St. Augustine. Specific to your question, it would not be in favor of preemptive military action. The first rule is: "We should do no harm to our neighbors." The "Just War" theory is about defending ourselves, about a greater moral good. What it does is puts parameters or boundaries around war so that the motives are right, the conduct is right and so on. But unless you're talking about an imminent attack, then it would be very difficult by the "Just War" theory to support preemptive military action.

34. How can the church support our nation's immigration laws but still show mercy and compassion to the aliens in our land?

There are three things that you have to consider here. First of all, Christians do need to respect the law (Romans 13). And if we make a law, we need to enforce it, or let's not make it at all.

Secondly, though, what do you do when people are already here? The Bible has a lot to say about hospitality to the foreigner. And I know people argue, "Well, they weren't talking about illegal aliens." Well, they didn't really have the border walls back then. They saw foreigners as people. And that's how we need to see them. I know some people see every illegal alien as a chronic danger. Some of them are criminals, and they need to be sent immediately back home. But in general, when it comes to the illegal aliens among us, there are two considerations.

First of all, to not meet their needs for basic health is wrong (Matthew 25:35-36). Many are children, for crying out loud. These are people. These are people God loves and Christ died for. So just because they're illegal doesn't make them less human.

The second consideration, though, is—and this is especially

important in Christianity—after somebody's done wrong, how do you help them do right? Christianity's not mainly a religion of punishment. It's a religion of helping people do what's right after they've done what's wrong (Galatians 6:1). And so that's what we need to consider. How do we help these people—even though they have done something wrong—find the path to what's right now?

35. If God is going to bring forth "a new heaven and a new earth," why should I care about environmental issues now?

We don't do what's right because it will last or because, somehow, it's going give us a great reward. We do what's right because God said to do it. It says very clearly in Genesis 2:15 that man's responsibility in the garden is to cultivate it and keep it, to produce from it and protect it. So while debate about how to best do that may never end, Christians need to do what we can individually, collectively and politically to care for God's creation. That is not up for debate. We do what's right because God said to do it. And God told us to protect the earth. Some people say, "If he's coming back real soon, why do that?" Well, if He is coming back real soon, you want to be doing what He told you to do. Obedience to God is the key.

36. Which important issues have been most ignored by the religious right?

There are several of them, really. 1) Poverty. The religious right simply says, "Let them lift themselves up by their own bootstraps! I earned my own way, why shouldn't they?" Some even believe they shouldn't try to fix the situation because Jesus said, "The poor will be with you always" (Matthew 26:11). His statement though didn't imply that individuals must stay in poverty throughout their lifetimes. Sadly, there will always be "newly" poor people. Christians must continue to find ways to effectively help individuals who are poor move beyond their poverty. Those who can should work. Government policy can be quite helpful in accomplishing that. 2) AIDS. There's an unfortunate attitude that says, "They brought it on themselves." But maternal fetal transmission, ignorance of the disease and rape prove that can be incorrect. 3) The environment. "God gave us dominion over the earth so we could take what we needed out of it." The first consideration concerning creation care can't be profit or loss, but rather what did God say to do?

All three of these issues have been—if not ignored— rationalized by the religious right to be secondary issues. But they are key biblical issues, and we need to do everything we can to relieve poverty, to heal the sick and to protect the earth.

37. Why are some Christians so aligned with Israel, while for other Christians, Israel is just one of the many countries that God cares about?

The answer to this question lies in your eschatology—how you view the end times. Many evangelical or fundamental Christians think that Israel as a country has everything to do with how the Lord's going to come back. They believe that He's going to come back to His holy land physically. And therefore, if we're not for Israel, and for them politically as they stand as a nation today, then we are against God because those are God's chosen people.

Other Christians are "amillenialists," and would say Christianity is not a geographically-based religion, that the nation of Israel is an important nation; but all of the other nations are just as important to God; that when Christ comes back, He'll come back for the whole world, no matter where He comes. Therefore, to love our neighbor as ourselves, we need not favor Israel above other nations. We need to treat all people with respect. Israel is a great land of our history, but it is no holier a land than any other place on the face of the earth because God made the whole world and has adopted into His chosen family, all those who believe in Him. Both of these viewpoints have a biblical basis.

38. Is it better to stay within a political group and work for change or to constantly re-identify with new groups and parties and their platforms?

It really depends on how you're wired. There are fixer-upper people, and there are pioneers. Fixer-upper people love to renovate things that are broken. If you love to renovate things that are broken, stick with your party and make it better. But there are also pioneers who like to build something new. And those are people who say, "Look, I've got to find a better vehicle for what the Lord's telling me is important." So you really could go either way. It just depends on how you're wired.

39. What's the biggest mistake a Christian can make with regard to their political involvement?

Well, that's easy. It's to use politics only to gain an advantage for yourself or your group and not to be a blessing to all the families of the earth. God made it very clear when He was forming a people, it was so that everybody could be blessed and not just the religious group that you happen to belong to (Genesis 12:3). So watch out that you're not using politics just as another way of getting something for yourself.

40. What is the most important focus a Christian can have when he or she is involved in politics?

I would say there are actually two focuses, and Christ named them in the Great Commandment: "Love the Lord your God with all your heart, soul, mind and strength. And love your neighbor as yourself" (Matthew 22:37-39). When you're involved in politics, do what you're doing for the sake of God as a reflection of His love, and, a reflection of your reverence for Him. Secondly, do what you're doing because you want to love your neighbor. You want to make his or her life better, and so that's why you're involved. And if you hold fast to the focus of both God and neighbor, you're going do great in the political field and make the world better for everybody.

TEN

"IN DEED":
A Workbook for Political Involvement

The future is purchased by the present.

—Samuel Johnson

A mericans have always been concerned about putting thought into practice. Some American Christians have, from the beginning, been concerned about the practicality of theology. Historian Daniel Boorstin writes of the Puritans, "Their orthodoxy had a peculiar character ... what really distinguished them in their day was that they were less interested in theology itself, than in the application of theology to everyday life, and especially to society. From the seventeenth-century point of view their interest in theology was practical. They were less concerned with perfecting their formulation of the Truth than with making their society in America embody the Truth they already knew. Puritan New England was a noble experiment in applied theology."[1]

This book concludes within that heritage. The United States government is an experiment in freedom. Christianity has historically been a central voice in that experiment. We hope our voice will contribute even more to the development of our representative democracy. If we look to the influence of the Holy Spirit rather than the force of government as our main means of improving the county, we will be most helpful. Government and religion have complementary roles. Both were instituted by God to help people live constructive lives. And there is a process that can help them work together.

For those who are ready to use The Pilate Process outlined in chapters six and seven and who desire to sharpen their punctuation skills as outlined in chapter eight, I offer the following pages. Herein, a Christian will find practical information to use in becoming competent in politics.

Basic References: My Government Organization

The following reference list can be completed with current and continually updated information available at www. statelocalgov.net. If you prefer not to use a computer, look in your phone book in the "Governmental Offices" section. This is not a homework assignment! Fill in only the blanks that will be helpful to you.

I. *Voter Registration*

Phone your board of elections or check the Internet to find out where to register. Make sure to update your information with the board of elections if you move or your name is legally changed. Go a step further: Suggest to your church leadership that they offer a Voter Registration Sunday periodically. It is easy to do and the local supervisor of elections will give you all the information you need.

II. *Neighborhood/Homeowners/Condominium Organizations, etc.*
   A. Name of Officer _____
      Address _____
      Email _____ Phone _____
   B. Usual concerns addressed: Neighborhood dues and uses of
      dues, neighborhood policies, input for improvement, etc.
      Go a step further: Attend community meetings and discover
      ways to "love your neighbor." Helping those nearest you is
      a first step in changing the world (Acts 1:8).

III. *School Board*
   A. County Office _____
   B. School Board (obtained by calling county office or
      checking Web site)
   C. Name of Contact _____
   D. Usual concerns addressed: Matters concerning local
      school curriculum, buildings, personnel, policies. Get
      involved to help, not to harangue.
   E. PTA President

IV. *City/Town Government*
   A. Important Department Phone Numbers
      1. Police _____ Emergency _____
      2. Fire _____ Emergency _____
      3. Administrative _____
      4. Public Works (streets, sanitation, etc.)
         _____
      5. Development (building, zoning, planning)
         _____
      6. Miscellaneous _____

B. Officials
   1. Mayor/Manager _____
     Address _____
     Email_____ Phone_____
   2. Commissioners_____
     Address _____
     Email_____ Phone_____
   3. Clerk_____
     Address _____
     Email_____ Phone_____
   4. Miscellaneous _____
     _____

C. Usual concerns addressed: Services such as police, fire, parks, libraries, streets, water, garbage, health protection, business regulation, zoning, etc. "Seek the welfare of the city" (Jeremiah 29:7). It is at this level that we can profoundly impact our local government and the cultural environment for our children and grandchildren.

V. *County Government*
  A. Important Department Phone Numbers
    1. Courthouse_____
    2. County Services_____
    3. Tag Offices_____
    4. County Commission _____
    5. County Attorney _____
    6. Fire_____
    7. Sheriff _____
    8. Miscellaneous _____
  B. Officials—Commissioners/Managers Contacts

Name _____

Email_____ Phone _____

Name _____

Email_____ Phone _____

C. Usual concerns addressed: County responsibilities such as education, parks, welfare, hospitals, health care, zoning, taxes, records, fire, police, environment, licenses, etc. Sometimes the zoning boards will be considering important values issues such as adult entertainment regulations.

VI. *State Government*

   A. Important Department Phone Numbers and Email addresses

      1. Governor's Office _____

      2. Miscellaneous _____

   B. Important Officials

      1. Governor _____

         Address _____

         Email_____ Phone_____

      2. State Legislators

         a. Representative _____

            Address _____

            Email_____ Phone_____

         b. Senator _____

            Address _____

            Email_____ Phone_____

   C. Usual concerns addressed: Education laws (major responsibility), public utilities regulation, highways, police and jails, welfare, health and hospital concerns, environment, business regulations, taxes, etc. It is at this level that important decisions such as protection of the traditional definition of marriage are addressed.

VII. *Federal Government*

  A. Important Department Numbers (toll free)

    1. Internal Revenue Service_____

    2. Miscellaneous _____

  B. Legislators

    1. Representative _____

      Washington office address _____

      _____

      Email_____ Phone_____

      Local office address _____

      _____

      Email_____ Phone_____

    2. Senator_____

      Washington office address _____

      _____

      Email_____ Phone_____

      Local office address _____

      _____

      Email_____ Phone_____

    3. Senator_____

      Washington office address _____

      _____

      Email_____ Phone_____

      Local office address _____

      _____

      Email_____ Phone_____

C. President _____

   The White House   Phone (202) 456-1414

   1600 Pennsylvania Avenue   www.whitehouse.gov

   Washington, DC 20500

D. Usual concerns addressed: Matters dealing with federal policy, such as taxes, foreign policy, federal law, human services, etc. There are continual issues to address at this level of government that have to do directly with biblical/moral values. Go a step further: Subscribe to a Christian Website that periodically alerts subscribers to important issues under consideration.

VIII. *Church—Political Concerns*

  A. Church Office _____

     Address _____

     Email_____ Phone_____

  B. Officials

    1. Pastor _____

      Address _____

      Email_____ Phone_____

    2. "Social Concerns" Leader _____

      Address _____

      Email_____ Phone_____

  C. Usual concerns addressed: Matters concerning our stewardship of God's world in His way, especially those of a direct Christian-political nature.

IX. *Specific Concerns Group (advocacy or interest groups having to do with areas in which you are specifically interested: abortion, sexuality, poverty, environment, justice, etc.)*

A. Group _____

    Address _____

    Email_____ Phone _____

B. Group _____

    Address _____

    Email_____ Phone _____

X. *Media References*

   A. Newspapers (contact information favorite or most irritating media)

     1. Name _____

      Letters to the editor address_____

      _____

      Email _____ Phone _____

     2. Name _____

      Letters to the editor address_____

      _____

      Email _____ Phone _____

     3. Name _____

      Letters to the editor address_____

      _____

      Email _____ Phone _____

   B. Radio Stations

     1. Station _____

      Address _____

      Email _____ Phone _____

      Program Manager _____

      Address _____

      Email _____ Phone _____

     2. Station _____

Address _____

Email _____ Phone _____

Program Manager _____

Address _____

Email _____ Phone _____

3. Station _____

Address _____

Email _____ Phone _____

Program Manager _____

Address _____

Email _____ Phone _____

C. Television Stations

1. Station _____

Address _____

Email _____ Phone _____

General Manager _____

Address _____

Email _____ Phone _____

News Coordinator _____

Address _____

Email _____ Phone _____

2. Station _____

Address _____

Email _____ Phone _____

General Manager _____

Address _____

Email _____ Phone _____

News Coordinator _____

Address _____

Email _____ Phone _____

Basic Resources: My Information Infusion

Being informed about political issues is relatively inexpensive and often, even free. And it is simple, but it requires regular discipline. The Internet offers all the information you need, along with your local library. Your local church can be a center for Christian political discussion.

I. *The Information Connection*

A. Newspapers: Widely available around the world in hard copy, most major newspapers are available on the Web as well. Study the issues in ways that television doesn't always allow. And God may use the up-to-date information that grabs our attention, to prompt us to pray about specific issues.

B. Periodicals: A spectrum of the more commonly accepted resources enabling Christian political involvement include:

1. Mainstream:
   a. *U.S. News & World Report* (www.usnews.com); *Time* (www.time.com); *Newsweek* (www.newsweek.com)
   b. *The National Review*; *The New American* (www.nationalreview.com) [conservative]
   c. *The New Republic* (www.tnr.com) [liberal]
   d. *World Press Review* (www.worldpress.org)

2. Christian:
   a. *Christianity Today* (www.cti.com) [evangelical]
   b. *The Christian Century* (www.christiancentury.org) [liberal]
   c. *Sojourners* (www.sojo.net)
   d. *Commonweal* (www.commonwealmagazine.org)

       e. *World* (www.worldmag.com) [evangelical]

C. *Congressional Quarterly* (www.cq.com): This is as close to an unbiased perspective as you can get. CQ examines important issues, informs of upcoming issues (so we may know in advance to write our representatives), and it reports how our representatives voted on the issues. It includes a fully functional collection of databases with user-defined search and reporting options that enables subscribers to track the movement of virtually every piece of news and all bills as they move through Congress.

D. Various books in the field of Christians in politics.

E. A resource librarian to help you find specific information you need.

II. *The Home Connection*

A. Television News and Specials: Though television journalism is thought to have anti-Christian bias in the name of being unbiased, it serves us all in several ways:

   1. Certain cable stations, such as C-SPAN, give uncommentaried, live coverage of Congress and other government action. Our reaction can prompt us to get involved.

   2. TV does tend to "confront" us personally with graphic portrayals of issues and well-choreographed programming; hence it provokes reaction. We need to turn reaction into involvement.

   3. TV makes us familiar with the most culturally popular issues and mind-set so that we can be realistic in our political approach.

B. Internet, newspapers and periodicals: All are affordable

to many families and can engender discussion within the family. Spiritual and civic concerns can be taught through family discussions of the facts.

C. Radio programs: Certain radio programs, from "All Things Considered" on National Public Radio to the most conservative Christian call-in programs, are available to raise our awareness. Many of these shows are podcasts available for download on the Web.

D. Discussions: Trading news and opinions with relatives, neighbors, and friends is still a potent means of being informed.

III. *The Church Connection*

A. Check to see if your church has any forum for Christian political dialogue. If not, perhaps God is calling you to pray about initiating that kind of addition.

B. Your church may have some sort of "semicolon discussion starter committee" charged with bringing political issues to the congregation. If so, what can you learn from them? What kind of follow-up is needed?

C. Your political leaning should look to a spiritual authority for its development. Your pastor is your chief shepherd, along with your church's governing board. Spiritually mature advisers help each of us implement God-given directions so if you desire to develop an idea or get biblical counsel about your concerns, talk to your pastor or designated "elder" in the Lord.

D. A trusted Bible teacher will help connect relevant biblical passages to your political concern. (If you don't have such a teacher, the church can direct you to one.) One of the basic questions for a Christian when it comes to any issue needs to be, What does the Bible say about this? Though sometimes the answer will be, Nothing specific.

E. Visit www.thechristiancitizen.net: This is a free tool to connect Christian leaders (pastors and others) with information they need to train their congregants and constituents how to make an impact politically on issues facing our nation, government, church and society as a means of spiritual witness and growth. You will find information that will link you point to point with the decision makers that can hear your concerns and influence the decision-making processes. Most importantly it gives you information so you can pray and be active in the community in a way that will bring glory to God.

Basic Questions: My Primary Concerns

Since some people would say that all issues and all candidates have direct religious implications, and other people would say only some issues or candidates have any direct religious impact, a few questions will clarify *your* calling.

I. *On Issues*
   A. Can this issue be found repeatedly in Scripture?
   B. What does this issue have to do with obeying God?
   C. What impact would a solution to this issue have on the lives of people? Whom will it benefit? Whom will it hurt?
   D. How much of my time should be spent on it?

II. *On Candidates*
   A. How does this person uphold biblical values?

    B. How does his/her voting record match Christian values?

    C. What is his/her personal example?

    D. What issues do his/her supporters prioritize?

    E. What is God calling me to do in response to this candidate?

III. On Self

    A. What are my motives when I address this issue/candidate?

    B. Am I afraid of something? Why?

    C. Am I trying to control something? To what end?

    D. From whom am I getting my opinion?

    E. Who is the beneficiary of my action? Me? A group? God?

    F. What can I learn from—and do for—the other side?

Basic Directions: The Lord in My Life

Keeping a record of the Spirit's leadings toward the political arena is a way of keeping ourselves accountable for follow-through. Here is one idea for such a diary.

I. Leadership resulting from Scripture reading and prayer

    A._____

    B. _____

    C. _____

II. Impending moral issues that can be referenced directly in the Bible

    A._____

    B. _____

    C. _____

III. God's leading for action; type of punctuation—! or ; or ?

    A._____

B. _____

C. _____

IV. *Actions taken*

A._____

Results _____

B. _____

Results _____

C. _____

Results _____

V. *Acts of Tolerance/ Reconciliation*

A. The other side's point is_____

B. The other side has a point when it says _____

_____

C. I can respect/serve the other side by _____

_____

VI. *Accountability*

Knowing I may need encouragement or guidance in participating politically, I will ask _____ to help me in this area of my Christian development.

Download this worksheet at www.rightwingwrongbird.com

ABOUT THE AUTHOR

Dr. Joel C. Hunter is senior pastor of Northland, A Church Distributed, an innovative congregation of more than 12,000 that worships concurrently at sites throughout Central Florida.

Interested in government since college, Dr. Hunter holds a Bachelor of Science in education (history and government) from Ohio University, a Masters of Divinity and a Doctorate of Ministry in culture and personality from Christian Theological Seminary.

An internationally respected pastor and teacher, he serves on the boards of directors for the World Evangelical Alliance, the National Association of Evangelicals, and the Global Pastors' Network. His wife, Becky, is president of the Global Pastors' Wives Network. They are parents to three sons and have been partners in the ministry since their marriage in 1972.

All author's proceeds will go to
Northland's future facilities